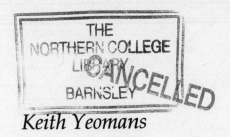

Keith Yeomans

Learners on the Superhighway?
Access to Learning via Electronic Communications

Winston Churchill Fellowship Report

NIACE
THE NATIONAL ORGANISATION FOR ADULT LEARNING

Correction

Please note that the ISBN number should be

1 872941 96 6

Published by the National Institute of Adult Continuing Education
(England and Wales)
21 De Montfort Street, Leicester LE1 7GE

Company registration no. 2603322
Charity registration no. 1002775

First published 1996

CATALOGUING IN PUBLICATION DATA

A CIP record for this title is available from the British Library

ISBN 1 872941 95 8

Printed in Great Britain by Antony Rowe Ltd, Chippenham, Wilts

Contents

Acknowledgements

The author thanks the Winston Churchill Memorial Trust for giving him the opportunity to undertake the research on which this report is based; Professor Brian Groombridge for supporting his application to the Trust; Professor Naomi Sargant for supporting his application and for her advice in preparing the report; Philippa Summersby for her support before, during and after the tour; the agencies and individuals in the UK who helped with contacts; all those who contributed to this study so readily; and the people across the North American continent whose generous hospitality helped make his stay memorable. Thanks are due also to NIACE for publishing the report.

Chapter 1

Summary

Background

This report is the result of a study-tour of policy makers and practitioners in electronic communications and education in the
United States and Canada undertaken by the author in autumn
1994.

Made possible by a Winston Churchill Fellowship, the tour was
designed to identify those policies, strategies and models of good
practice in increasing access to learning via electronic communications relevant to the UK and European environment with a view
to promote them in the UK and Europe.

The Superhighway as a Threat to Access

The argument is made in the report that, while the superhighway
is promoted as a means of improving access to learning opportunities, it could prove to be the opposite unless intervention takes
place in its design and implementation.

It is also argued that the issues surrounding its development as
essentially a commercial communications environment are especially difficult to understand in the public service culture with
which people in Europe are familiar.

Access and the Technology

Key concepts in information and communications technology
(ICT) are briefly outlined as a basis for understanding the com-
mentary.

The origins of the conventional idea of access to education are
briefly discussed and related to the changes in communications
infrastructure now taking place on both sides of the Atlantic. It is

argued that these changes are radically influencing the realisation of this idea.

Five factors affecting access to learning are identified, and related to the role of ICT:

- **location**: the extent to which, for example, learners in poor or rural areas will be reached by the superhighway
- **user cost**: the amount the end-user will be expected to pay for hardware, software, learning materials and line charges
- **content relevance**: the extent to which electronic learning materials and services will be available in the marketplace to serve the needs of minorities and disadvantaged groups
- **competence**: the importance of competence in the technology's use in determining both users' access to resources and providers' ability or inclination to make them available
- **awareness**: the role of individual and organisational consumer awareness as a force in building an equitably accessible superhighway.

An analysis is made within this framework of the policy and practical interventions observed at state, regional and national level in both the private and public sectors. These are critically reviewed within each category for their relevance to the UK environment.

An Agenda for Policy-makers

The implications of these findings for policy-makers, for research and for learning-related governance are briefly set out, followed by suggestions for an agenda to promote equitable access to learning on the superhighway and help develop fully its use for education and training in the UK. These are:

Awareness-raising: an awareness-raising programme should be designed and implemented by national and local government, education and training agencies and providers, professional associations, trades unions, learners' representative organisations and the relevant media to ensure that decision- makers at all levels understand the issues affecting access to learning via ICT and their ability to influence them.

Audits: institutional, local and regional audits should be carried out of existing and projected (over the next five years) needs and resources in electronic learning, quantifying demand, stimulated where appropriate by public sector incentives and contributing to the process of awareness-raising.

Strategies: these audits should be used to develop strategies at those levels designed to maximise the benefits and minimise the cost of ICT-based learning to end-users. Although focused on learning, the strategies should be cross-sectoral, especially at regional level, to ensure synergy and congruence between, for example, the objectives of local education authorities, TECs, economic development departments, universities and companies.

Cross-sectoral Initiatives: these strategies should be used by potential stakeholders to evaluate the relevance and feasibility of the growing number of initiatives in this area and, where appropriate, to encourage them and direct them towards meeting access-oriented goals.

Consumer Power: learning providers and users should use the information gained through audits and awareness campaigns to negotiate with ICT suppliers on, for example, favourable tariffs and special services for disadvantaged groups, as far as regulation allows.

Campaigns: organisations representing the interests of learners, educators and disadvantaged groups should take on the responsibility for finding out about their constituents' needs in this area, how these needs are met by suppliers and the regulatory agencies, and, where appropriate, mount campaigns to ensure that they are fairly served.

Public Sector Pioneers: those agencies and institutions who have ICT capability should, where appropriate, take a lead in marketing it to public and private sector users in their localities as a means of driving down costs and spreading awareness and competence.

Product/Market Development: the communications industry at all levels should make full use of cross-sectoral partnerships and opportunities to work with disadvantaged groups and those representing them as a way of developing user-friendly mass and niche market products and of growing markets. Government agencies should consider ways of facilitating these relationships. Industry analysts and managers should focus on the particular management features and information economy conditions, including the intellectual property rights environment, which favour profitable indigenous and local production.

Local Learning Networks: learning providers at local level should use their audits and strategies to consider ways of developing effective, self-financing local learning networks and materials in cross-sectoral partnerships to ensure that due access is available to the wealth of learning resources at this level and that the infrastructure exists to enable full-scale local communication between learners and teachers.

'Big Switches': institutional providers, especially in higher and further education, should evaluate the potential of collaborative ICT-based production and distribution systems at regional, national and international levels as a way of reaching non-traditional learners and achieving economies of scale.

The Global View: development agencies should evaluate the role of ICT in the areas with which they are concerned and consider ways in which the expertise available to them conventionally and electronically can be exploited to enhance their work.

The Media: should continue their move away from an uncritical embrace of the superhighway and its traffic to extend the attention they have begun to focus on questions of equity and social justice in electronic communications.

Government: should review the means available to it for promoting these goals through national regulation, in concert with industry and at local and regional level through carefully designed, monitored and evaluated initiatives.

Chapter 2

Introduction

Access to Electronic Learning: The argument

Learners of all kinds are being promised a great deal by the champions of the information superhighway. 'Virtual campus' and 'classroom without walls' are common metaphors for the new technology's ability to carry text, graphics, video and voice to and from anyone linked to this global network.

Lifelong learners, in particular, stand to benefit from services which make high quality education and training available 24 hours a day at home, at work or wherever they choose to study. Transnational delivery of these services makes job mobility easier. The technology makes possible the complex management information systems needed to allow individual learners to wend a path through education, vocational and non-vocational training and between jobs, accumulating a record which will be their passport to continuing employment.

It is not surprising, then, that the European Commission's Information Society vision, now crystallising as the dominant model of economic growth and governance in Europe for the beginning of the twenty-first century, lays great store by electronic learning.

Vital Decisions for the Education and Training Communities

During the next five to 10 years the international communications industry plans to invest billions of pounds in developing a global infrastructure based on fibre optic cable capable of carrying massive volumes of digital information in interactive multimedia form. Governments at every level from local to supranational and their regulatory agencies are trying to find ways of harnessing this revolution.

Decisions are being taken by politicians, regulators and industry planners which will shape the information society for years to come. Some of these decisions will have a direct bearing on access to electronic learning. It is vital that the education and training communities at institutional, local and national level are aware of the issues surrounding these decisions and their implications for the future of learning so that they can play an active part in making them.

The Danger of a Widening Gap in Education and Training

There is a great danger that, far from bringing the benefits of interactive multimedia education to a wider range of learners, the superhighway will widen the existing gap between educational 'haves' and 'have-nots' unless steps are taken to make it open to all and to offer the products and services available on it at widely affordable prices.

This report is an attempt to identify those steps and suggest how they may be taken by learners, educators and trainers in the UK to ensure that electronic learning is available to everyone who could benefit from it.

Its conclusions are also relevant to policy-makers outside the UK. Left to market forces, superhighway development will widen the gap in provision not only within countries but also between them. The principles outlined in this report apply equally to inner cities and rural areas in Europe and north America, to the poorer countries of Africa, Asia and Latin America and to the small island states of the Caribbean and the Pacific. Solutions in those countries may, however, be harder to reach as their governments hold little sway over the communications industry and the short-term business case for infrastructure development is often weak.

Electronic Learning: The technology

The term 'electronic learning' is taken here to mean any learning process (in school, post-compulsory education, at home or at work, vocational or non-vocational, at any age) which involves electronic communications. It also covers here not only their use as an instructional medium but also as a way of communicating accreditation data, administrative information, guidance and support for learners.

Electronic communications technology includes radio and television (whether delivered by satellite or terrestrially), computing, telecoms, and electronically processed print (desk top publishing and reprographics, for example). More particularly, the term includes the recent, converged forms of these processes now familiar as applications and systems such as interactive multimedia and telematics (the combination of computing and telecoms). Some of the key elements of these processes are outlined in Chapter 3.

This technology has received much media coverage in the past two years, and there can be few people who have not encountered at least some of its vocabulary. In its broadest form, information technology is also now so pervasive a part of our lives that it would be very hard for anyone in an industrialised country to pass a day without coming into direct or indirect contact with some of its applications: a supermarket till, a gas bill, a telephone call, a car made largely by robots containing microprocessors to regulate its performance, driven in an urban traffic system whose flow is controlled by computerised traffic lights and monitored by video camera – the list is long.

A Limited View

Although it impinges so much on our daily lives, this vast, complex system of systems is hard to understand for all but a few engineers, enthusiasts and scientists. It is presented to us, and we relate to it, mainly as particular applications: a computer games machine, a cash point, a cheap international telephone call. We are encouraged to take this view because we experience the technology mainly as consumers who are being invited to buy its products and services.

In education, as in other fields, discussion of the technology tends to centre on the cost of buying/replacing a desk top computer, what is the best application for a particular job and, increasingly, the recurrent cost of using on-line services via the Internet. Often the technology is depicted as an alternative to human effort, and discussion rages around its comparative effectiveness in particular situations.

Unfulfilled Promise

Education has long been used as the pristine banner brandished at the vanguard of each new advance in communications technology. Radio, television in its terrestrial, cable and satellite forms, computing, advanced telecoms have all been promoted to an unknowing market and electorate as ways of delivering better education to more people. Sometimes the promise has been fulfilled. More often it has been quietly discarded and forgotten as old movies replace health education programmes on the broadcast schedules of both rich and poor countries and video games sell faster than courses in French.

The Limitations of a Project-Based Approach

Faced with this elusive promise, the education and training communities, among others, have responded by mounting projects to help explain and promote the technology's role in learning. Although an important contribution to organisational change in many areas, these projects, usually publicly funded with some commercial contribution, tend to be capital intensive and short-run, with outcomes inadequately evaluated and disseminated.

They can be limited in their prognostic value because they depend on unrealistic levels of resource and often mask implementation costs vital to long-term success. Sometimes they are counterproductive in raising unrealistic expectations and antagonising non-participants by diverting resources away from other priority areas. There are also ethical issues in public/private projects about the extent to which public money is being used to fund research and development whose benefits are mainly enjoyed by commercial partners.

The Role of Policy

Product-, project- and vision-driven approaches to electronic learning, whatever their strengths and weaknesses, all tend to obscure the strategic issues which are now and in the short-term dominating the direction it takes. Decisions about public and commercial policy now being taken are the Capability Brown to our electronic communications landscape. They not only affect what we see and where we walk now but, once taken, will determine the paths and vistas of generations to come.

The policies now being framed, remote and complex in themselves, will have a direct and practical impact on the potential for electronic learning. They will influence, for example, the charge for a telephone call, the range and availability of on-line services in rural and inner city areas, the type of electronic learning products and services available to consumers and the price they will pay for them.

To this extent these policies are the proper concern of everyone in the education community, from individual learners through teachers and heads, principals and vice-chancellors to local, regional and national policy-makers.

They should be of particular interest to those in the educational community and to politicians who are concerned with promoting wider access to learning, especially for disadvantaged groups. This priority is now reflected in the Government's commitment to extending lifelong learning.

The strategic approach is not new. It has been followed by the major communications companies who are the prime movers in the revolution and, in some cases, by the more farsighted departments of local, national and international government. Electronic information policy has become a field of academic study, notably in the UK by the Programme on Information and Communications Technology (PICT), though education has significantly attracted less interest from researchers until recently.

The Need for Greater Awareness

These deliberations, however, receive little public or professional attention. The issues they raise tend not to be communicated in forms accessible to teachers or parents or adult learners or managers, who find themselves constantly reacting to new products, new services, new threats and opportunities without any context for interpreting them beyond 'I want one,' 'I can't afford it,' 'I don't understand it,' or 'how will it affect my job?'.

The need now is to make planners and users aware of how to actively influence the technology's implementation in ways valuable to them; to bring electronic learning, together with other public service functions, into the remit of consumer awareness so that suppliers, customers and those outside the commercial electronic marketplace all benefit.

The Report

This report is aimed at policy-makers rather than information and communications technology specialists for the reasons given above. A basic understanding of the technology is, however, necessary to appreciating its educational and social impact.

Chapter 3 includes a brief account of the main concepts relevant to understanding the technology's impact on learning.

Chapter 4 contains an exploration of the issues affecting access to education via the technology.

Chapter 5 is an account of the north American policy and practice in electronic learning observed on the study tour, from state/province to national level. The experience of particular sectors at each level is reviewed and an attempt made to show its application to the UK environment. Reference is made in **bold type** to individual contributors listed in Appendix 1.

Chapter 6 contains the conclusions drawn from this analysis and some suggestions for an institutional, local and national agenda.

Appendix 1 contains profiles of the contributors to the study listed alphabetically and by level and sector.

Appendix 2 is a list of the documents given to the author by contributors and held by him.

Chapter 3

The Changing Technology

To understand the issues relating learning to information super-highway (ISH) development it is vital to grasp the basic concepts underlying the technology: bandwidth, digitisation and interactivity.

Bandwidth

Bandwidth refers to the information-carrying capacity of a distribution system, whether it be traditional twisted-pair telephone wires, coaxial cable, fibre optic cable, a satellite transponder or a terrestrial transmitter. The capacity needed increases with the complexity of the information sent. Voice telephony and slow speed data transmission require only narrow bandwidth, while moving image video and high speed data need broad bandwidth. The ISH is generally accepted as denoting broadband capacity.

Digitisation

This is the process of transforming audio, video, text and other forms of data (now including instructions to remote machines and smells) into electronic pulses expressed in a digital form (usually binary) so that they can be captured, stored, manipulated and distributed faster and with less bandwidth than their analogue equivalents. A related technique is compression: squeezing a video signal, for example, so that more material can be sent down a narrower bandwidth.

Interactivity

This is the capacity to exchange information in both directions. Telephone systems are inherently interactive. Cable, satellite and terrestrial transmission systems are typically unidirectional, though most are now capable of some two-way traffic. The relative value and volume of this traffic in each direction lie at the centre of strategic commercial and regulatory battles now being fought in north America, the UK and, to some extent, worldwide.

With digitisation as the key to large-scale electronic information processing the facility to carry this out apparently depends on access to bandwidth with interactive capability. There is, however, another factor: time. A CD ROM allows the user a high level of interactivity with a great deal of material but it does not take place in real time. The necessity for full-scale interactive broadband communications is at present determined by the demand for simultaneous communication of equal volumes in both directions. Once the capability is easily available it will be used more generally, however.

There are now few uses which demand this capability. Videoconferencing and high speed data exchange are the most obvious, but the market for them is limited. In spite of this, the US cable industry claimed to be laying fibre optic cable at 100 miles an hour and the telecoms companies are pouring billions of dollars into similar holes in the ground. This investment is an act of faith, a belief that the income derived from uses yet to be developed will repay the investment now being made.

The economic forces shaped by these factors are determining the price, content and availability of electronic learning in ways to be explored in the next chapter.

Chapter 4

Access to Education

The Changing Idea

'Access' has come to have a particular use in education, as in broadcasting and disabled people's rights. This use refers to the ability of disadvantaged groups, often minorities, to gain access to a widely available service. Access courses have helped people without traditional qualifications enter higher education; the broadcasting access movement (which gave rise to Channel 4) was intended to give public voice to opinions and experiences not normally heard in mainstream broadcasting; access for disabled people means the facility for them to use independently, for example, buildings or public transport. Parallels can be drawn between these trends and the participatory politics of the 1970s.

Implicit in this use is the idea of a service to which most people do have access. The idea stems from our experience in the UK over more than a century of steady movement towards universal service not just in education (through, for example, the 1870 and 1944 Acts) but also in broadcasting and telecoms. All three institutions have been shaped to deliver (arguably) the same level and quality of service to people throughout the UK. Broadcasting and telecoms, in particular, have been regulated and engineered so that people living on the wrong side of Scottish mountains and in central London pay the same licence fee and telephone charge rates and enjoy the same (there are exceptions) range of programmes and telephone line quality in spite of the massive cost differences in supplying them.

Although the changes of the past 13 years have radically altered this approach to service delivery, the notion of universality is still a strong, if sometimes unrealised, influence on the way anyone over the age of 40 sees the world. The prevailing view of access to education is framed by this perspective. It is of little help and may actually be counterproductive in achieving social justice in electronic learning under the conditions now being created. Attention is drawn to the contrast between this view of universal access and

13

the individual, user pays model emerging in the new media by Naomi Sargant in her distinction between the provision of education through 'large and public' providers like institutional education and broadcasting on the one hand and 'small and private' provision on the other, characterised by open and distance learning, narrowcasting and interactive multimedia applications.[1]

Education is increasingly being seen by some policy-makers as a sector of the information economy. Traded information forms a dramatically rising proportion of the wider economy, especially in richer countries.

The growth in information trade is largely driven by the expansion of electronic communications, as expansion in manufacturing was by the steam engine. Governments worldwide, including those of the US and the UK, are reshaping their media and telecommunications regulation to allow this trade to increase according to *laissez-faire* principles. The debate in the US is over the extent to which universality will be abandoned in conquering cyberspace. This issue has hardly yet been raised in the UK, where it is just as relevant. Whatever the debate, it is more than likely that the global information economy will be based on a free market dominated by the user pays principle.

The notion of access predicated on universal service will not apply in this environment. Access to education will be governed by a very different set of constraints, to the extent that learning is absorbed into the economy of electronically traded information. These constraints are considered below.

A further assumption behind the conventional view of access is the existence of a discrete body of 'education' to which it refers. This view has always been challenged by the participatory approach in which learners' interests and needs influence provision. The interactive capacity of ICT and its role in bringing education into the marketplace will accelerate this process: a change whose benefits and disadvantages will, to some extent, be determined by the intervention of traditional educators.

Factors Affecting Access

The emerging US experience, echoed here, is that access to learning through ICT will be much more differentiated between individuals and groups than access to conventional learning provision. Existing factors such as aptitude, availability, awareness, income and location will be made worse and overlaid by new, technology-based factors. These factors will not only relate to learners but providers: a 'double dip' disadvantage because no one can have access to learning resources which are not being produced.

The irony of this view is that, with certain exceptions, access to learning may actually be made more difficult by the wider use of technology claimed to be able to improve it. This contention cannot, however, be used as a reason for avoiding use of the technology, because those teachers and learners excluded from it will become increasingly marginalised from an information economy whose wealth generation, intellectual as well as material, grows more dependent on it.

The evidence for this argument is set out under five headings which are offered as the basis of an approach to understanding access to learning via ICT. These are:

- awareness – are both users and providers aware enough of the technology and the issues surrounding it to make effective use of it and ensure its widespread availability at an affordable cost?
- situation – is the technology available at the site where learning takes place?
- user cost – can the learner afford the hardware, software, line and other costs of learning in this way?
- content relevance – are the available learning products appropriate to the learner's needs?
- competence – is the learner sufficiently competent in the technology to use it effectively and is the learning provider competent enough to teach and make learning materials available in this way?

These factors are not new. They also shape access to conventional learning. But their significance is now more critical when applied to ICT issues.

Awareness

Access issues grouped under this broad heading may be related to both users and providers. It may seem too obvious to need stating that people cannot use a service unless they are aware of it. Yet pre-competitive ICT initiatives are often application- rather than user-driven. Promotion to target groups rarely appears as a budget item. Educators, trainers and librarians are all familiar with the lonely PC sitting in a corner of some public space waiting to be used. Professionals are all too often unaware of electronic information services available to them whose cost has already been met by their organisations.

Consumer awareness by both users and providers is of greater concern. Wide differences can be seen between here and the US. These apply more to networked services than to IT products, which are seen as belonging in the marketplace. Contributors to the study have suggested that the difference may partly be explained by the long tradition of active consumerism in the US and by the relatively recent arrival of competition in UK telecoms, a service which middle-aged managers have grown up seeing as a state monopoly. Another factor may be the sheer complexity of options available in the new technology. Even apparently simple choices between e-mail services require a quite sophisticated technical grasp. But as the range of choices in hardware, software and systems increases individuals and organisations will find it increasingly necessary to find out how to make the best buy.

Educational institutions may find benefits in pooling knowledge and collaborating in negotiations with service suppliers, as in the US, to achieve the best deal for themselves and their clients. The level of informed awareness needed to act successfully in this way requires a careful investigation of needs and resources as yet unfamiliar to most managers and planners. Unless it is achieved, however, users and providers of learning will be disadvantaged in the market for electronically traded information.

A consciousness of the need to intervene to ensure equity of access is the most important factor under this heading. Much of the publicity surrounding the ISH and the public discussion flowing from it assumes that it will develop in conditions favourable to widespread access: general availability, low/no cost, content abundance and user-friendliness are all heavily promoted. It should be clear from the brief account of barriers to access above that this is far from the case. Two months' exposure to parallel publicity and discussion in north America suggests that public service managers as well as campaigners are more aware than most of their UK counterparts of the danger to equity of access to the ISH in their own field and of the action needed to remove it.

Situation

The single greatest claim for ICT is its ability to collapse space and time, making learning resources available to people in remote rural areas. A long tradition of distance education in the US bears testimony to its value even when delivered in print. The state Public Utility Commissions were set up early in the century to ensure that people living in rural areas were not denied access to telephone services. A current debate in the US on whether ISH regulation should specify 'universal service' or 'universal access' has powerful implications.

This analysis directly affects the degree to which situation is a barrier to access. Cable and telephone companies operating in a relatively free market are less likely to run interactive broadband cable and the applications supporting it to areas where use will be limited. The profitability of a cable run is a function of the number of subscribers reached and the volume of business they will generate against the cost of laying the cable. Rural areas are disadvantaged by this formula, as are poorer urban areas where not only levels of spending but also credit ratings are deciding factors. The **Center for Media Education** has already run a campaign against 'redlining:' the practice, followed by some services in this country, of refusing to supply or surcharging for services to particular areas whose residents are a credit risk.

Not only residents but also businesses, colleges, libraries and schools in rural and low income areas are suffering from this approach to infrastructure development. One senior analyst interviewed for this study voiced the concern that it would cause further social tension in inner cities by widening the knowledge gap of young people there and, thereby, their ability to escape from the poverty cycle. In a similar way, concern was expressed at the **Pacific Telecommunications Council** that the Pacific islands will be left out of the global information society because their relatively small populations and low income levels will mean that they are bypassed by the global infrastructure now being built.

The importance of situation is complicated by what has become known in the US as 'the platform debate' between the cable, computer and telecommunications companies. Regulation has led to each industry sector investing in systems with different characteristics. Telecoms has traditionally offered low bandwidth, low user end cost and high real time interactivity. Cable has delivered high bandwidth, low user end cost and low interactivity. Desktop computer based systems have offered high user end cost and high non-real time interactivity.

While all three are converging as quickly as regulation and the business case allow, they are all still in competition, trying to make sure the superhighway is suitable for their traffic. A key factor in this competition is whether they make their money from 'black boxes.' According to one leading commentator from a computer industry background, the driving force in competition is 'bootstrapping': the ability of service providers to drive demand. On this basis, computers sharing a common architecture and linked by telecoms are a network in themselves.

The estimated 35 per cent of US homes with computers installed, of which 15 million are connected to modems and five million subscribe to on-line services, form a critical mass which is driving interactive multimedia developments. In response the cable companies are, according to one industry expert, 'adding intelligence' to their networks by, for example, developing interactive services based on servers supplied to them by computer companies.

This battle of the Titans may seem far removed from the needs of low income lifelong learners in rural or inner city areas but becomes more directly relevant when the effect of its progress and the outcome on institutional and individual outlay is appreciated. The difference between the high entry cost of a platform-based approach and the low one of subscribing to value added services significantly affects the decisions of not only individual learners but also institutional and public sector planners intervening on their behalf.

Location will remain a major determinant of these services' relative availability. The cyberspace map in 2000 will not be a neat pattern of hubs connected by sweeping broadband superhighways but a mixed topography where affluent cyber suburbs are served in this way, while isolated cyber hamlets and virtual ghettoes lie at the end of dirt tracks. Nor will virtual topography resemble the terrestrial version: as one authority pointed out, Australia is a small village in cyberspace.

User Cost

The cost of hardware, in particular, continues to fall both absolutely and relative to capacity. One industry contributor cited Moore's Law (named after Gordon Moore, the founder of Intel) which apparently asserts that in computing value as a function of price and performance doubles every 18 months, claiming that this had been so for the past 30 years. Against this value curve must be plotted the growth in both hardware and software obsolescence, surely an essential feature of computer industry growth and one whose impact is complex. One software developer estimated that a significant technology change takes place every six months: faster than his company can get products to market.

Whatever conditions affect the industry, the cost of buying hardware and software remains a major barrier to its use by institutions and individuals in both north America and the UK. Calculating the size of the problem is also difficult. Overall estimates of computer ownership and software sales are of little help: questions have to be asked about specific use capability. How many homes, schools, women, for example, have easy access to equipment capable of running interactive multimedia products? Those hardware and software companies who sell mainly to the domestic market (computer games manufacturers, for example) often make dedicated equipment which cannot run wider applications. Their diversification into the home education market should be closely watched by educators.

The price and availability of products must be left to the mechanisms of the marketplace, it will be argued. Both the hardware and software sides of the computing industry are relatively unregulated compared with their cable and telecoms counterparts, who peer enviously out from between the, admittedly bending, bars of their public service regulatory cages. There may be room for what one leading US policy analyst described as 'market confirming mechanisms' in the regulatory repertoire but direct intervention, apart from anti-trust action, seems unlikely.

Cable and telecoms companies argue that they can reduce the cost barrier by transferring much of the cost in the learning site to the virtual capacity of their servers and databases. But experience on both sides of the Atlantic suggests that home and institutional users are nervous of writing an open cheque to on-line suppliers. This inhibition may disappear with familiarity but is currently one factor affecting the use of virtual capacity.

There is also a disturbing lack of transparency about the actual cost of on-line services. A great deal of effort has gone into promoting the Internet as a paradigm for the ISH. Claimed to be free, unregulated and universally accessible, it sets fair to join Coca Cola and chewing gum as an icon of the American way of life. But the torrent of positive journalistic coverage is already being questioned in the US.

The Internet evolved from an earlier communications network originally developed by the US Defense Department to allow data communications to be rerouted if part of the network was destroyed. It was later augmented by an academic and scientific research network funded by the National Science Foundation. The principles on which it operates are the essence of Vice-President Gore's ISH vision.

As traffic on the Internet increases, its expansion is increasingly being subcontracted to the communications industry. This has raised questions about access and control among US communications pressure groups, concerned about the future use of what has so far largely been a publicly funded resource. Although the Internet is, in principle, infinitely expandable and so not a finite resource like the waveband, its architecture and protocols are determined by its developers. Access to it is also monitored centrally and controlled largely by commercial access providers, for example, America On Line and Compuserve.

There are already signs of strain in the free, unregulated, accessible model. Stories have emerged of access providers using price control to manage excess demand and of 'traffic jams' in busy sectors. As its potential for commercial transactions is more widely appreciated, the demand for greater security and for ways of logging transactions is growing. Nor can the existing network cope with the projected demand for wider bandwidth from interactive multimedia use.

Expansion investment in the Internet will be concentrated in those areas most likely to yield a commercial return. While the public service dimension by which it is now being heavily promoted worldwide is unlikely to disappear, it may become increasingly marginal. Radio started in the US as a largely unregulated two-way communication between equipment owning amateurs. Regulation arose in response to the recognition of the spectrum as a valuable commercial commodity. Today's net surfers may become tomorrow's ham radio operators: a relatively small band of enthusiasts confined to a narrow slice of the 'spectrum' whose communications are tightly controlled.

How will education fare in this process? The answer is as yet unclear, but the question no less important. Educators and learners, like other user groups, are being encouraged to see the Internet as a panacea for their electronic learning needs. Far more will have to be known about its development and about the future cost of the services to which it will give access before large-scale learning systems are predicated on its use.

On-line service charges and telecoms tariffs will become as important an element of user cost as hard- and software are now, to the extent that value added network services and virtual capacity take over from desk top storage. Tariffs and charges are much more of a campaigning issue for educators in the US than in the UK because there is more scope to influence them, and, some contributors to the study argued, because there is a longer and wider tradition of consumer militancy there.

Although the UK telecoms regulatory environment is in some ways more competitive than that in the US, there is, so far, less opportunity to negotiate charges with telecoms suppliers. A long tradition of public sector monopoly provision has left the abiding impression that they are beyond consumer control.

Student support is a vital issue in user cost. Electronic learners in the US are often funded by their employers or by education loans. The electronic education community has fought hard with legislators to ensure that students taking their courses are eligible for public support, recognising this as necessary not only to achieve equity but also to finance the technology's development. As demand in the UK extends beyond full-time, on-campus academic higher education, fuel will be added to the fight to gain similar support for Britain's home-based learners.

Content Relevance

'Content drives' according to one US cable industry executive. This view that people will not subscribe to a cable system or on-line service or buy a computer unless it gives them access to entertaining or useful information is the truism which fills high street shelves with software packages and prompts cable and telecoms companies to acquire film and TV companies in order to gain access to their product. It is the dynamic behind the rapid growth of companies like Microsoft and the bubbling ferment of 'garage' multimedia houses in California.

It is also the rationale behind the non-commercial bulletin board systems and specialist user groups spawned by the Internet to cater for a range of leisure, political and social tastes.

But learners will only join the superhighway if it carries material relevant to their needs in an accessible form. This requirement is well understood in north America, where a combination of vocal minorities and market-sensitive providers has resulted in an awareness of the need to create appropriate learning resources for different language groups. Jones Cable's research into the interests of ethnic minorities in inner cities is one example.

To the extent that it exists, the interactive multimedia environment presents problems to content providers. The development costs of an interactive multimedia product are in the region of £50,000. In a predominantly free market how can an income be derived through the control of intellectual property rights (IPR)? Broadcasters and publishers make sense of their balance sheets to their financial stakeholders through, on the one hand, advertising or the licence fee and, on the other, through unit sales. How can rights holders show a return on a system which offers no control over the integrity of property offered on it nor any means of monitoring its use? Under these circumstances content providers are cautious about entering cyberspace. Indeed, the contractual environment it creates is inimical to the concept of property rights as expressed in Anglo-Saxon law.

Regulators for the US Administration are conscious of the need to build an IPR framework conducive to promoting the interests of educators. Faced with a similar problem earlier in the century the manufacturers of British radio receivers negotiated the licence fee as a means of generating an income to produce the programming that would help to sell their equipment. Licensing agreements persist in the educational use of computer software. Shareware is a cheap alternative, but, for that reason, is unlikely to attract the rights holders of much attractive material.

Vague and abstract though they may seem, the principles of ownership of electronically transmitted information are a vital component of the user cost equation and, thereby, of the access debate. Vital, too, is the need to understand the extent to which these principles are determined by multinational providers whose decision-making criteria are remote from those of educational administrators.

The economics of electronic information trading are far from widely understood outside the multinational companies who rely on them to run a business. Yet they are one of the greatest forces shaping the future of electronic education. Public sector policy-makers need to be aware of them and of the impact they have on commercial strategy.

Competence

The inability to use ICT acts as a barrier in several ways. Incompetent learners are not only barred from the rapidly increasing volume of material available electronically but may also be inhibited from taking part in courses which feature it. A less obvious but no less important barrier is that of incompetent providers. One of the educational advantages of interactive multimedia is that they can be produced and adapted locally, as opposed to conventional broadcast and published materials.

Some of the most interesting material being produced in the UK and in northern America either originates in school and university learning resource centres or is produced centrally, with the capability of being suited to local learning needs via authoring tools. These processes devolve control to teachers at local level who inevitably become gatekeepers for these materials. Their inclination to create or mediate them will depend to some extent on their fluency with the technology. This state of affairs is acknowledged in the initiatives on both sides of the Atlantic to promote wider use of ICT in the curriculum and to extend professional development in this field.

Competence in both users and providers is affected by a range of cultural, personal and socio-demographic factors including relative access to the technology, age, aptitude, disability, ethnicity, gender and language. Research at the Open University, for example, into the effect of these variables is contributing to an understanding of the extent to which they form a barrier to access.

Gaining competence should not, however, be seen as a one-way process. The technology is beginning to be seen as a cultural form dominated by the English language, literate (as opposed to oral) codes and male-oriented applications. It will need to be adapted to the needs of current non- and low user groups to spread effectively beyond these cultural confines.

At a wider level, it has been argued (by a major software producer among others) that the appearance of personal computers on middle managers' desks in the 1980s changed the perception and role of IT in the organisation and that this transformation has yet to take place in education. Senior educators unfamiliar with or ill-disposed towards ICT may be less likely to sanction its implementation.

Note

1. Sargant, N. 'Choosing to use the media', *BUFVC Handbook for Film and Television in Education, 1991–2* , p4.

Chapter 5

Promoting Access via the Superhighway

The Relevance of the North American Experience

These barriers to access are being tackled, not always consciously, at different levels in north America. Most interventions affect more than one barrier. Some, like the quick recourse to litigation in the US, are less appropriate here. The lessons outlined below are those which seem most likely to survive the Atlantic crossing. Many have, or are soon to have, UK parallels and may, therefore, serve as useful comparisons. They are ranked from local to national, though in relating them to the UK environment it is necessary to be aware of the extent to which the constitutional and actual power of the individual state lies someway between local and national government in the UK, varying with the function described. Key interventions at each level are summarised and an attempt made to apply them to the UK environment.

State/Province Government and Public Sector Agencies

Context

The US states have had a great deal of control over telecoms. Some of the effort behind the new telecoms legislation being debated in Congress was directed towards eroding that power in order to make regulation more responsive to the interests of the regional, national and multinational companies who deliver it.

The states' influence over education is also much greater than that of federal government as, apparently, it was not covered in the constitution. This may in some way be seen as the reverse of the UK situation, where local control of education is decreasing while telecoms is increasingly being sold competitively in the local marketplace.

Under the current pattern of regulation some of the most signifi-cant developments in ISH access are taking place at state level.

Strategic Plans

Prominent among these are the educational technology plans pro-duced by the states in response to relatively modest federal project funding requirements (see **US Department of Education**). Often incorporating sophisticated analyses of needs and resources, these plans have allowed states to create a framework in which in-formed decisions can be taken by public and private sector organi-sations about individual and collaborative action.

The information contained in them forms a basis for negotiation with suppliers, as well as assessment of future needs, while their preparation and dissemination has helped promote awareness of the issues surrounding education on the ISH to managers and the public. In some cases this has lead to changes in state accounting systems to create the budget structure needed to deal with elec-tronic communications. One of the most ambitious approaches at this level is the California State Government's SB 600 Task Force on Telecommunications Network Infrastructure, with a brief to look at the needs of schools, public libraries and community cen-tres (see **Far West Lab**).

Many state Public Utility Commissions, who set telecom tariffs, are apparently thinking about moving education from a business (*pro rata*) to a package rate, while Tennessee and Texas have cut rates for schools.

Some states (Utah, for example) have taken a cross-sectoral ap-proach to planning, based on a vision which extends across all ar-eas of economic and social development.

UK Application. The disaggregation of institutional education into local management of schools and incorporated colleges, to-gether with increasingly competing higher education institutions, makes the case, ironically, even stronger for strategic planning at local level to ensure that equipment and services are compatible, that efficiency can be achieved through economies of scale and that lifelong learning goals can be more effectively achieved through greater transparency between providers.

As the national information infrastructure begins to take shape and the services on it become available there is also a growing need here, as in north America, for a set of yardsticks by which to measure the utility and value of this increasingly complex range of information products. Based on an analysis of needs and resources, these strategies can be used as yardsticks. They also add strength to negotiations with suppliers.

The case for local plans is even stronger in the UK, where government policy has focused telecoms competition at local level, offering greater opportunities for customers to benefit.

Pioneering Public Sector Use of the ISH

Some agencies and institutions have been encouraged to use the ICT resources they have developed not only for education but also to play a pioneering role in providing services to other public sector and commercial users. This not only yields revenue but also fosters important cross-sectoral links.

MCET's status as a quasi-state agency allows it to broker with other state agencies. It has formed a corporate development function to market its facilities, including videoconferencing, and has deals with, among others, the body responsible for Massachusetts' airports, ports and toll roads.

On the other side of the Union in Hawaii, PREL has plans to put education in the lead agency position as ICT service providers to business and government.

UK Application. While there are at the moment more opportunities in the US for educational institutions to broker advanced telecoms services (videoconferencing, for example) changes in both the technology and its regulation are beginning to extend the same opportunities.

To the extent that institutions are both local network nodes and centres of expertise in the technology's use they may play an important role in promoting it to the wider community. The universities' position in relation to JANET is one example. Institutions gain by spreading the cost and maximising the use of the technology, as well as by building relationships with potential customers for their other services.

Cross-sector Partnerships and Initiatives

States have also served as the appropriate environment in which cross-sectoral partnerships can develop. Hawaii was often cited as the exemplar of this approach. A combination of the administrative and commercial isolation resulting from its geographical remoteness (2,000 miles from mainland USA), its island culture (a phenomenon similar to Singapore's) and its far-sighted state government have resulted in the rich seam of strategic public service and cross-sectoral initiatives outlined under **Hawaii State**, **PREL**, **PEACESAT** and the **Pacific Telecommunications Council**.

One original example, based in Hawaii, is the partnership under the Star Schools programme including **PREL** and the Ohau Wireless Cable Company. Under this arrangement the company is licensed as an educational provider and provides both the television output and the hardware for schools to receive it via a microwave link free of charge. The company buys back 80 per cent of the airtime to sell commercially while PREL provides the programming. Profits are shared between the partners.

In California, **Computer-Using Educators, Inc** and the **Industry Council for Technology in Learning** are both active forums in which educators and the communications industries can identify and work together on common goals.

UK Application. Although there are now several public/private sector partnerships in this field in the UK the model is still in its infancy and few have fully addressed ways in which commercial involvement can be used to extend access by spreading costs.

As with any link between public resources and private profit, great care has to be taken in ensuring that public benefits accrue and that tax payers' money is not simply being used as venture capital. Public sector participation should be on the basis of open and well-informed decisions directed towards specified outcomes. With these caveats, joint ventures of this kind can provide the necessary synergy for innovative and successful projects in the field of electronic learning.

There is also a strong case for developing local links between educators and the communications industries, based on a mutual need for dialogue between users and producers in a fast-changing industry and marketplace. Such relationships help promote access by increasing awareness and the availability of appropriate products.

Local Learning Networks

Both **MCET** in Massachusetts and the **Open Learning Agency** in British Columbia are prominent examples of plurally-funded, state/province-wide multimedia learning providers whose local focus enables them to concentrate on the particular needs of their target audiences.

UK Application. Local learning materials production declined in the UK as higher education and LEA budget cuts affected educational television services and deregulation eroded local educational broadcasting. New opportunities are now emerging as cable companies offer local TV channels and telecoms services and the technology offers an opportunity for local authoring and reauthoring of multimedia learning materials.

These opportunities merit careful consideration by local education providers. They can extend access by enabling providers to target the needs of disadvantaged groups more closely.

Tariff Negotiation

Because the state has traditionally been the strongest regulatory tier for telecoms lobbying, the industry is often orchestrated at this level. **MCET**, for example, has succeeded on its own behalf in arranging a short-term cheaper rate with Nynex. See also **CCSSO** and **WCET**.

UK Application. There is less scope under current UK telecoms regulation to negotiate favourable tariffs. The regime is changing, however, and the variety of services offered on the superhighway will greatly complicate pricing.

It is vital that local education authorities and institutions become aware of the extent of their power as consumers to influence the price and provision of these services, especially to the disadvantaged groups for whom they have a responsibility.

Regional Public Sector Activities

Context

There were some signs of a growing interest in supra-state regional activity, particularly in western USA and Canada, some of it influenced by the North American Free Trade Area (NAFTA).

The four regional organisations visited, **Far West Lab**, **Pacific Region Educational Laboratory (PREL)**, **PEACESAT** and the **Western Cooperative for Educational Telecommunications (WCET)**, however, predate this development.

Some of their activities overlap with those already mentioned as taking place at state level, but are separately noted here because the relationship between these regional organisations and their constituents is significantly different. The laboratories are autonomous, with activity-oriented links to institutions, while WCET is an association of universities.

UK Application. The regional ambit of activity is also becoming more important in the UK (analogously) because of European Union influence, the new regional tier of national Government service delivery and the severance of grant maintained schools' and further education colleges' links with local education authorities.

This means that the regional tier is a fertile one for access-oriented, cross-sectoral initiatives in electronic learning. The role of higher education, particularly given the concentration of ICT capacity and expertise on university campuses, the sector's growing interest in serving local communities, and its independence from traditional public sector boundaries, adds strength to this movement. Communications industry licence areas are also rarely coterminous with local government boundaries, making them easier to fit into regional perspectives.

Audits

Some schools in California have carried out audits of their ICT needs and resources, including staff development and other implementation costs, as a first stage in developing a strategy. The **Far West Lab** has played an important part in piloting this approach and developing suitable analytical methods.

As with audits conducted at state level, the process of conducting an audit in this area is vital, not only in quantifying needs and resources as a basis for negotiation with suppliers but also in raising awareness among practitioners and policy-makers of the issues involved in developing the technology's use in learning. On both counts the audit process is an important tool in promoting access.

UK Application. It has already been argued that audits are important in all tiers of planning. Their value at regional level lies in the strategic, cross-sectoral view which can be obtained. Data can be collated more effectively at this level not only from local education authorities and other local government departments but also from grant maintained schools, FE colleges, universities, health authorities, national government agencies and the private sector.

Consumer Power

In spite of the competitive environment, institutions at all levels have for some years now recognised their shared interests and come together to lobby various constituencies. It is quite common for them to negotiate with telecoms service suppliers for favourable tariffs on the basis of aggregated demand. Five Colleges Inc, a non-profit group in western Massachusetts, was formed for this purpose. The **Far West Lab** plays a leading role in mobilising schools' and school districts' energies in lobbying not just service suppliers but also state government. Institutional audits are a vital tool in this process.

WCET lobbies not only national and state agencies, including teaching unions, on issues such as loans for distance learning students, but also its own membership of 150 universities to promote greater awareness of the issues and practices surrounding electronic learning and the means needed to implement it successfully.

UK Application. Because the balance of ICT regulation and supply between national, regional and local levels is different in the UK it is harder to transpose this tier of intervention. Telecommunications tariffs, for example, are largely regulated at national level, though this may change. Cable companies and radio stations deliver at local level, are regulated nationally but form part of regional, national or multinational agglomerations.

Regional inter-institutional and professional associations also have a role (following WCET's example) in promoting consumer awareness among their members.

Regionally informed and led lobbying can, however, can have considerable power to the extent that it transcends the particular interests of individual players and allows the larger guns of wider interests to be brought to bear. It may also have particular relevance for Northern Ireland, Scotland and Wales.

Post School Distance Learning

Context

Distance learning has long been thought to meet several access criteria: it makes education available to people living in remote areas; it extends the range of provision by spreading scarce expertise more widely; it can lower delivery costs by increasing the student/teacher ratio. These benefits apply whether the delivery technology is broadband cable or the post. They have long been at a premium in the US, where a low population density has combined with a popular ethos of achievement through education.

UK Application. While distance learning may not be rooted in the national consciousness to the same extent, the emergence of the Open University (OU), in particular, in the UK has raised awareness of the value of this approach to learning. Open and distance learning methods are gaining greater currency as ways of extending lifelong learning.

A major difference between the approach in the two countries is the extent to which the monolithic OU has dominated electronic distance learning in contrast with the US pattern of association. As more and more conventional post-school institutions embark on distance learning in the UK, this federal approach offers some advantages. While US institutions are at least as competitive as their UK equivalents, they have found benefits in collaborating in this area.

'The Big Switch'

One variant of this collaboration, the **National Technological University (NTU)**, has been described as 'the big switch.' From its small office block on the outskirts of Fort Collins, Colorado this tightly-run organisation orchestrates the relevant courses of all its affiliated universities across the country into an electronic and print-based academic programme e-mailed and beamed by satellite across the US and internationally.

A commercial company, Mind Extension University (M/EU), part of the **Jones International** cable group, adopts a similar approach across a wider curriculum base and aimed at a less specialised body.

One advantage of large-scale ventures like this is their ability to make economically feasible provision for minorities. M/EU, appreciating that inner cities form an important sector of its potential market, has carried out research into the needs of the ethnic minorities living there as a basis for aiming provision at them. A similar and equally commercial position is taken by the **Distance Education and Training Council (DETC)**, who argue that the market led approach of their members allows them to develop carefully targeted courses at lower cost than conventional institutions enabling them in turn to cater for market niches.

There are some instances of collaborative ventures in electronic higher education (the Higher Education Funding Council's Teaching and Learning through Technology initiative, for example) but they are largely confined to campuses. Some higher education institutions are experimenting individually or in local areas with cable companies.

The access premium of collaboration in delivering economies of scale and extending the reach of teaching resources seems obvious and, therefore, a model to promote. It was not possible in the time available to evaluate this argument but an impression was formed that the reality is more complex.

The economic and logistical ability to meet minority needs – a key access feature – does seem more firmly rooted in practice and makes the case for inter-institutional collaboration.

These large, virtual institutions are expanding into a global market and have Europe in their sights. While the prevailing electronic learning environment in the UK, combined with the cost of culturally re-engineering some courses, have reduced the threat of immediate competition, there is no room for complacency in the mid-term.

The Annenberg/CPB Project

This non-profit/public sector agency's unique position spanning broadcasting, publishing, telecoms and institutional education allows it to play a significant part in raising awareness among higher education planners and practitioners of the changes being wrought to learning at this level by the technology.

UK Application. In spite of the wealth of innovation in electronic learning now being promoted by the BBC, British Telecom and the

OU, as well as at local level, there is room in the UK for a version of the Annenberg/CPB Project to develop and disseminate thoughtful policy and practice spanning higher education as a whole on the one hand, and, on the other, the converging communications industries.

National Campaigning Organisations

Context

The necessity of raising professional and public awareness of the issues surrounding access has already been argued. It should be clear from the few examples already mentioned that this process is well advanced in the US at local and regional levels, especially among institutional educators.

The need for intervention at national level, in response not least to the Administration's deliberate attempt to stimulate public debate, has been successfully met by a number of small and, mainly, non-profit organisations.

Non Profit Agencies

Prominent among these are the **Benton Foundation**, the **Center for Media Education** and the Electronic Frontier Foundation, who have focused considerable energy and expertise on identifying the issues in the superhighway debate which affect individual, community and civic access to and rights in cyberspace, and have extensively promoted these issues through the media. Groups of key public and private sector leaders have been brought together to tackle ways of promoting equity and safeguarding the needs of minorities and the disadvantaged on the superhighway.

Professional Associations

Within education **The Council of Chief State School Officers** is an excellent example of a professional membership organisation which, having identified the issues relating to its constituency and formulated a clear and coherent strategy for resolving them, lobbies politicians, regulators and industry from its Washington, DC base while informing and engaging its membership at state level.

UK Application. It is in this area that the gap between the US and UK experience is most glaring. The issues are very similar. Their appreciation and the research supporting it are as advanced in the

UK as in the US but are confined largely to a small section of the academic community, individual educators and journalists.

The UK Government and its regulatory agencies are, like their American counterparts, engaging in consultation exercises. Media coverage of superhighway topics (though so far not access issues) is now as widespread here as in the US. The difference lies, as far as it is possible to tell from the inevitably skewed perception formed in a rapid tour of US opinion-formers, in the extent to which UK organisations representing substantial professional, public and voluntary sector constituencies are themselves aware of the issues, see them as a priority at senior management level and have any vision of how these issues relate to their constituents or how they may be favourably resolved.

Several reasons have been offered for this disparity. It is tempting to speculate about differences in consumer culture and the communications environments in the two countries, but that is beyond the remit of this report.

As in the US, major decisions are being made over the next few years about the creation and regulation of a pervasive infrastructure which will greatly impinge on our lives and those of succeeding generations. The issues surrounding these decisions are complex, some of them demanding a detailed knowledge of communications technology. But their importance outweighs these difficulties.

It should be a priority for the senior management of professional associations, trade unions, statutory authorities, institutions, voluntary organisations and commentators on education and related areas of social provision to make themselves aware of the impact these issues will have on their area of work, to develop strategies for surviving in and exploiting the new environment and to disseminate those strategies to everyone who can play a part in implementing them.

Much of the information and intelligence needed to do this is readily available here. The task lies in moulding it into a form which is readily understood and easy to translate into effective action.

The Communications Industry

Context

The companies visited ranged from communications industry giants like **Jones International** and **Microsoft** to small, creative houses like **Ingenius**. While tensions may sometimes arise between the need to make a profit and the needs of learners and educators for affordable services, their interests often run parallel in the shared need to raise awareness, develop competence and meet particular needs. This has led to a spate of local initiatives by, among others, the telecoms companies (**Bell Atlantic**, for example).

Professional Support

The cable industry, far richer than its nascent UK equivalent, boasts contributions like **Cable in the Classroom**, with its teacher support incentives and network, and the **J C Sparkman Center**'s teacher training work, both combining real educational benefits with effective public relations and good marketing practice.

Product Supply

The role of Microsoft and interactive multimedia courseware suppliers like Ingenius and The Curriculum Network in fostering access is perhaps less obvious but no less important in the longer term. Their commercial objectives demand an approach to education as revolutionary as that of Paulo Freire in that it transcends conventional administrative and institutional boundaries and challenges teachers' hegemony over learning.

Access equity issues do arise over intellectual property dominance and pricing in relation to their products, but the desire of companies like these to sell effective products to broad-based markets is a growing threat to any bastions of elitism in conventional learning. It also poses profound questions about the spatial and temporal organisation of learning which lie at the heart of the access paradigm.

Product Metering

One interesting attempt to unravel the user cost/product supply knot which inhibits both product supply and access to it is the software produced by **Vistar** for community learning utilities. By metering product end use the software is intended to allow electronic information to be treated like electricity, gas and water, lowering entry cost for users and offering to suppliers a means of ensuring a return on their products. There was not time to see the system working during the tour, but it is generating considerable interest on both sides of the Atlantic.

UK Application. There are UK industry parallels to most of the initiatives mentioned above. To some extent, this is not surprising, as the UK cable industry is dominated by Americans.

One of the most salutary lessons for UK educators is the extent to which the superhighway and the traffic on it is, firstly, global in scope and, secondly, American in conception and ownership. The challenge for the UK, to be hardened or softened by regulation yet to be set in place, will be to retain a distinctive identity in the form and content of electronic learning products available on the superhighway.

This challenge is difficult to appreciate from the historical perspective of a rich print and electronic media landscape, dominated by institutions like the BBC, the OU and Penguin and underpinned by a universal, publicly-owned broadcasting and telecommunications system. Seen from the effervescent 150-acre Microsoft campus or the small offices of a minute but fast-moving interactive multimedia producer the challenge is real and imminent.

In this context the access issue becomes that of being able to learn from a product or service which is not only readily available, attractive, easy to use and educationally effective but also has strong cultural references for the user.

This view should not be taken as cultural isolationism or the false belief that British cultural products are in some mysterious way 'best.' It is, rather, the argument that, to the extent that learning is contextually dependent, its effectiveness may, in some cases, be influenced by the familiarity and relevance to the learner of the resources used.

While the talent to create powerful interactive multimedia learning resources exists in the UK and is to a large extent actively employed, the challenge lies in harnessing it to production and distribution systems designed to prosper in the new, fast-changing information economy. This demands an approach to venture capital and information product markets as yet less evident here than in the US.

Federal Government Departments and Agencies

Context

In a country where suspicion of government at all levels is deeply rooted and in an area of activity so dominated by industrial actors, the 'big idea' for the ISH appears to have come from the Administration and has led to substantial federal involvement. The extent to which this involvement was driven by the goal of maintaining equity of access to the new communications environment was also surprising to an outsider.

There was not time in the course of my Fellowship nor is there space in this report to examine the historical and constitutional reasons for this anomaly but an impression was formed that telecoms as a universally available service: 'Ma Bell,' helping to bring the nation together this century as the railway did in the last, occupies a similar place in the public imagination to that enjoyed by public service broadcasting until recently in the UK. Certainly, the ubiquitous, reliable US payphone, almost identical whether framed by palm trees in Hawaii or tucked out of the wind in a Chicago street, has become through film and television as much of an icon as the Coke bottle or the baseball cap.

It remains to be seen, however, whether the equity principle can be asserted by any of the constitutional levers available to American society or whether it will be eroded as quickly as its British broadcasting counterpart in the 1990s.

Research and Development

Most directly relevant to this study are the measures taken by the **US Department of Education**, not least the appointment of Linda Roberts as Special Adviser on Technology in recognition of her strategic work on electronic learning at the **Congress of the United States Office of Technology Assessment (OTA)**.

A clause in the 1994 Goals Act calls for planning on technology and makes provision for grants to states to undertake this. While these grants are relatively small and the Department's influence on a predominantly locally run system cannot be compared with that of its UK equivalent, they have nonetheless concentrated administrative minds at state level and downwards into, for example, school districts, resulting in some impressive plans. These are helping educators at all levels to come to grips with the elusive task of evaluating the technology's future impact on their work and making provision for it. Vital, too, is the Department's role in producing a national vision and in lobbying the **Federal Communications Commission** to regulate favourably for schools.

The OTA's role in supporting this work through applied research is also of great importance. One aspect of this is their search for 'productivity hooks' – applications of the technology seen by teachers as helping them to do their job better.

These education-specific activities fit well into the wider context of the National Information Infrastructure initiative, based at the **US Department of Commerce**. The role of the Telecommunications and Information Infrastructure Assistance Program, though broader based, is parallel to that of the Department of Education in using relatively limited resources to encourage local agencies to focus on key elements of equity-oriented development, for example user-driven applications, increased civic participation and private sector investment.

Key concerns underpinning the Program are the creation of incentives for infrastructure provision in economically unattractive areas (the 'last mile problem') and a more differentiated telecoms tariff structure which discriminates in favour of schools and other public service users. The Program is also keen to promote consumer awareness in telecoms.

UK Application. Since the visit took place, several initiatives by UK Government departments and agencies have been announced which resemble those mentioned above. The Department for Education and Employment's Education on the Superhighway scheme, the Department of Trade and Industry's Multimedia Special Interest Group and Oftel's consultation documents are among the most prominent examples.

There has also been much, though so far less critical, media coverage of the UK superhighway's promise. Signs are appearing that its development is becoming an active political issue. The considerable European interest and resource, focused in its Fourth Framework activities, should also be taken into account.

Given this level of involvement it may be thought that few lessons are to be learnt from north America. There is one significant exception to this comfortable view: the strategic role of local and regional government. It has been suggested in this account that US state governments, stimulated by federal programmes and legislation, have so far played a leading role in stimulating equity-oriented, cross-sectoral activity and as a focus for campaigning and strategic planning.

Even given the constitutional differences between US states and cities and UK counties or metropolitan authorities, there is still a great deal of unrealised opportunity for similar activity, especially as telecoms competition has been configured at local level to a much greater extent than in the US. There are similarities in population and economy size between many states and local government areas.

Some British local and regional authorities have made comprehensive, cross-sectoral plans for electronic communications, often driven by educational and economic development goals. There is, however, still much scope for progress both in terms of awareness and strategic planning. As in the US, central government can play a part in stimulating thoughtful and effective action by offering incentives linked to clear guidelines for planners.

There is also much scope for greater transparency in national policy making, linked again to a higher level of professional and public awareness of access issues in superhighway planning. Oftel, for example, has shown itself open to consultation on changes in telecoms regulation affecting the education community but it remains to be seen whether the level and quality of response from that community will be as thoughtful or as strongly expressed as its equivalent in the US.

International Agencies

Context

Politicians and industry spokespeople now commonly draw attention to the global dimension of the superhighway and its handmaiden, the Internet. Most of the major communications companies are, or aspire to being, global players. Yet the bulk of regulation and, therefore, the focus for lobbying and strategic planning, is at local or national level. The International Telecommunications Union and the European Commission's Telecommunications Directorate are obvious exceptions to this, while the 1995 pronouncements of G7 are an indication of change.

Development

Three of the agencies visited exemplified good practice in developing international planning and intervention in improving access to education via electronic communications, especially for poorer countries. The **Pacific Telecommunications Council** and **PEACESAT** both had a regional remit covering a vast geographical area scattered with islands, some extremely poor, for whom telecoms can make a real difference in educational and economic opportunity, and surrounded by some of the richest, most technologically advanced countries in the world. **The Commonwealth of Learning** has an even wider remit, though half the Commonwealth's member states are islands.

UK Application. As a member of the European Union and the base for the Commonwealth, the UK is already locked into two supranational tiers of decision-making in the economic, educational and social use of telecommunications.

There is, however, scope for the international aid agencies based here to acquire a greater understanding of telecom's role in development and to take a stronger stand in campaigning to ensure that the superhighway does not pass only the doors of the richest inhabitants of the global community and in devising ways of preventing the world's poorer inhabitants from becoming even further marginalised by its arrival.

Individual Experts

Professor David Farber, Rob Glaser, Professor Robert Harris, Dr Meheroo Jussawalla and **Dr Catherine Murray** have all made, and continue to make, substantial contributions to the development of the superhighway and its use for education. They operate in widely different areas and offer contrasting views on the ways and means of managing it for the public good. It is impossible to generalise from the variety and depth of the individual insights they offered. Several strong principles and acute observations, however, stand alone and are worth careful consideration:

- Australia is a small village in cyberspace

- the proportion of money spent on communications has remained constant since 1900
- civil liberties should also exist in cyberspace
- an understanding of the dynamics of the changing information economy is essential to survival on the superhighway
- regulation can be counterproductive if it is carried out by people who do not understand the technology.

These individuals were in regular contact, as were others visited, with their counterparts in the UK. There is no shortage of expertise and experience in this field. The difference, and this is only impressionistic, may lie in the level of public profile given to these analysts and commentators.

Chapter 6

Conclusions

A Difference in Awareness

The greatest relevant difference observed between north America and the UK lay not in the availability or use of the technology but in the level of informed awareness by practitioners and policy-makers at all levels of the issues, needs and resources relating to equitable access to the ISH by the educational community and by disadvantaged groups in general.

This awareness and the intelligence underlying it were due in part to the extent of the public debate stimulated by the Administration and in part to the information gathering undertaken in response to, mainly, federal government initiatives. They were also due, arguably, to the prevalence of a consumer mind-set in relation to the communications industry of longer standing and stronger voice than is typical in European public service-influenced regimes. They also derived, it was suggested by several contributors, from the emphasis on social equity in the US constitution and its reflection in the country's law and institutions.

This emphasis, expressed through agencies like the state Public Utilities Commissions, is under a great deal of pressure from the communications industries, now in a global expansionist phase estimated to double their value in 10 years' time. Regulatory requirements for universal access and/or service would greatly increase the cost of building the infrastructure.

Will this awareness and activity make a difference to the future of learning by disadvantaged groups via the ISH? If so, what lessons can be transferred to the UK and to other environments?

Investment, Regulation and Access

The ISH itself and its alleged prototype, the Internet, are both heavily promoted in the US and in the UK as widely accessible and pluralistic in the traffic they carry. It was clear during the tour and has become clearer since that this is an idealistic and misleading vision, not only in north America but worldwide.

ISH development is taking place in an increasingly deregulated environment. Although the technology's novelty attaches a high degree of risk to the hundreds of billions of pounds being invested internationally in the infrastructure, this largely corporate capital naturally seeks evidence of a return. Investment, already nervous of heavy regulation, is also demanding conditions favourable to the development of revenue-bearing traffic and a clearer idea of what that traffic may be.

In practical terms, this means that broadband systems will only be built in areas where the volume and value of demand for its traffic is apparent. It also means that, far from being the open, free cyberspace zone vaunted by its early proponents, the ISH will be a tightly managed trading zone whose capacity is not limited by technology but by commercial strictures. Public regulation will be replaced to a large extent by commercial regulation. This is already evident in the case of the Internet, where access and capacity demand are being price-regulated, and expansion is being geared towards commercial use.

Learners wanting to use the ISH to gain access to high quality, multimedia resources and the interactive capability needed to make their learning effective will have to live in an area rich enough to be passed by it and be rich enough themselves to afford the higher charges linked to these more sophisticated services.

This difference will apply not only within countries but also between them. It was clear from visits to international agencies concerned with the Pacific islands and developing countries worldwide that poor countries had good reason to fear that they would be bypassed by the ISH because the cost of including them in the global infrastructure would not be met by prospective revenues.

It may be argued that this inequity is only another instance of the unequal distribution of any resource and should not, therefore, attract special attention. But it is now argued by information economy specialists, including several contributors to this report, that the ISH will further polarise inequities in wealth to the extent that traded information becomes a dominant element of the global economy.

Public Education and Commercial Electronic Learning

It is also clear from the tour that electronic learning, though likely to grow into a substantial sector of the information economy, will be treated as a commodity rather than a resource. To the extent that education is still treated in most countries as a public good, largely funded by the state as an investment in national prosperity and culture, there is political pressure to make it as widely available as possible.

But the potential ubiquity of electronic learning means that public education may become only one, and not necessarily the largest, customer in a marketplace which includes corporate clients and individual home consumers. While this change may have the benefit of increasing the overall investment in learning products, broadening their content base and making them more user-friendly, it is also likely to price them out of the reach of many who would benefit from them.

The issue here then becomes not the ISH's role in extending the reach of the existing education system but rather its role in transforming it to a market driven industry. In this scenario the policy concerns for the education community are not how they may afford the technology to extend their existing work, but how they will support its use for learning by disadvantaged groups and retain a significant influence on the educational content it carries.

It is not suggested in this vision that public education will disappear, nor that a premium will no longer be placed on high quality conventional private education. It seems more likely that a growing amount of public and private expenditure on education will be drawn into commercially driven, electronically delivered learning systems over which public sector educators will have little control.

In these circumstances academic institutions and individuals would move from their traditional role of controlling the content, organisation and delivery of learning towards a service contract with learning corporations in which they supply the content and accreditation of products whose development and distribution are determined by market forces.

Another perspective in this rather bleak vision shows rich consumers of education continuing to enjoy the benefit of regular, close contact with eminent scholars and talented teachers while their poorer counterparts in inner cities and rural areas are fed a basic educational diet through some form of electronic learning system, watched over by minimally paid and qualified 'learning assistants.'

Policy Implications

The Need for Intervention

These speculations, based not only on impressions gathered during the tour but also from work in the UK and elsewhere, are offered not as serious attempts to predict the future but as a bid to stimulate the debate within the educational community on the development of electronic learning and that community's continuing role in it. The extent to which they become a reality depends partly on the community's active intervention in the development and control of electronic learning systems at local, national and international level and partly on the market for learning products.

The Role of Research

To be effective, policy at all levels will require a much clearer view than is now generally available of the actual costs and benefits of these systems and products as they evolve.

The most important outcome of the tour was the brief insight into the attempts at state and institutional level to quantify these for current and projected levels of penetration. This exercise is now more practicable than before as a picture emerges of applications and systems and their rate of availability over the next few years. It is still complex, however, and, to be successful, should draw on the methods and intelligence used by the communications industry to plan its products.

At a more fundamental level, there is a need for public sector research, drawing on the techniques of information economics, into the value of electronic learning products and services. The factors affecting this value include:

- the rate of redundancy of the information they contain
- the cost of gathering, storing and distributing it
- the size of the market for these products and services
- the costs of reaching that market
- the price the market will bear
- the intellectual property rights environment shaping products, costs and markets.

These factors, it will be argued, are no different from the ones affecting the commercial viability of any product. This may be true, but the way in which values are assigned to them has been radically changed by the emergence of new electronic capture, storage and distribution techniques.

Broadcasters, computer software suppliers, local education authorities, publishers and telecoms operators all have their own methods of assessing the value of the information in which they trade and the systems by which it is traded. But as these industry sectors converge and transcend conventional relationships with their markets these methods are changing. For example, a great deal of effort is going into exploring ways by which information rights holders, whether they be authors, institutions or publishers, can cover their costs or make a profit from interactive multimedia products distributed via an intelligent telecoms network. The fruits of this effort will determine the design, ownership and volume of vehicles travelling on the superhighway and, to a large extent, where and how they are built.

At present, research into this area is largely confined to a few communications companies and research agencies. It is not even, in the author's experience, widely used in some sectors of the communications industry to inform product and service development nor is it widely used in public sector education policy formation. Yet it is impossible for effective policy decisions to be made in this area without a clear understanding of the dynamics of the electronic information economy. Attempts to do so will perpetuate the reactive posture of public sector decision-making and ease a transition to the pessimistic scenario outlined above.

The wider sharing of this expertise and intelligence is inhibited not only by its unfamiliarity but also because much of it resides within companies and is treated, quite reasonably, as commercially sensitive information. The north American experience suggests two solutions to this:

- the public sector should make wider use of academic work in this field within the public domain
- public bodies should form strategic relationships with commercial organisations which allow the sharing of this type of information to be mutually beneficial.

Public/Private Partnerships

These public/private consortia have now become established as vital organisms in the ecology of electronic learning. It has already been suggested in this report that public sector agencies, in order to gain the maximum benefit from them for their tax and rate payers and to act as good stewards of public resources, must have a clear idea of what they bring to the relationship, what outcomes it is likely to yield and what their share of those outcomes should be. This, once more, calls for the level of well-informed strategy evident in some of the areas visited in north America.

Professional and Public Awareness

This expertise should not only be available to public policy-makers at all levels but also, in an appropriate form, inform professional and public debate. The constraints outlined here which are determining access to learning via ICT (and, therefore, to an increasingly important element of learning opportunity) will only be relieved if there is widespread popular support for action along these lines.

This means a programme of dissemination and awareness-raising directed, in the first instance, at the education community and also those public and voluntary organisations and politicians who are concerned with the well-being of disadvantaged groups. Electronic learning, it should be clear from this account, cannot be seen in isolation from the other public service traffic on the ISH.

Informal transatlantic links already exist between some of the contributors to this study and their counterparts in the UK and in mainland Europe. The scope for these relationships and exchanges should be extended and the platform for their discussions broadened using the technology itself.

The media have an important role to play in this process by engaging in a level of coverage and debate, as they have already shown signs of doing, which extends beyond the 'toyshop' approach to ICT into a more mordant analysis of its potential impact on learning.

Consumer organisations and pressure groups also have a part to play in stimulating, as their north American counterparts already do, a critical awareness among the public and among relevant occupational groups of the real economic choices to be made, not only between the technology's products and services but also in its planning, development, availability and impact.

The International Perspective

This report and the study tour on which it was based have focused on the relevance of the north American experience to the UK. The experience of international agencies contributing to the study and the author's experience in other regions suggest that the principles, issues and models outlined here have a universal relevance.

It is equally clear that successful solutions demand the local inflexion of a set of resources and networks whose control lies increasingly outside the remit of individual education administrations. The American business maxim 'Think global, act local' applies increasingly to learning management.

A New Constitutional Framework

The north American experience demonstrates dramatically that equity of access to electronic learning cannot be achieved by attempting to impose the old conceptions and structures of public service regulation on the new organisational forms emerging from the development of electronic communications technology.

Equitable access will be achieved to the extent that these tensions can be successfully resolved in new constitutional forms. Research into and debate around these new approaches to governance is already taking place at a general level. The educational community should enter more fully into this process and its outcomes should be related to electronic learning.

The principles remain the same but the challenge is to find new ways of applying them and new forms in which they can be enshrined in time to ensure the technology's use for the greater good. One key example of this is the principle of universality which has dictated the development of broadcasting in the UK and of telecoms both here and in the US. It is most unlikely to be applied to the ISH map in the prevailing economic and political climate. Yet universal availability of learning products and services is a basic requirement of equitable access.

Some consideration has been given here to various partial solutions to this dilemma: public/private partnerships, for example, which may soften the blow by spreading infrastructure development costs and underwriting some learning service revenues. But these are only partial solutions and very context specific.

Another approach receiving consideration directs effort towards ensuring that educational products and services can be translated across different distribution media so that learning sites not passed by the ISH can gain access to equivalent alternatives. To be successful, this approach demands a very clear view of the learning objectives the technology is to be used to attain, as well as a good grasp of its capability.

Solutions like these depend upon a detailed appraisal of the local communications ecology as well as of wider trends. The importance of promoting access by adapting both infrastructure and content to local needs is often overlooked in the emphasis on national and global communications in ISH publicity. As the technology is largely owned and managed by multinational companies and as the development cost of its commercial products and services is still relatively high this emphasis is understandable.

But the same technology has a unique capability for intercommunication at any level provided its networks are appropriately configured and the means are available. With the exception of the local television and radio initiatives of the 1970s, educational resources have generally been published nationally or internationally. Yet educational theory and practice support the principle of starting from the known and familiar and working outwards. This approach is especially important, it can be argued, for disadvantaged groups.

ICT offers an unparalleled opportunity to have the best of both worlds: high quality interactive multimedia communication at local as well as interpersonal and global levels. It would be unfortunate if the chance of creating local databases and resource banks, underscoring the traditional strengths of local education authorities in the UK or small island states, were missed in the race to send e-mails across the world. An innovative approach to the development and regulation of ICT networks and content at local level, exemplified in some of the north American local learning networks and public/private partnerships, is essential to creating the critical mass necessary to achieve this key feature of accessible learning.

A Special Case for Learning?

Most of the issues and initiatives reviewed in this report apply broadly to ISH access for disadvantaged groups in general. Several of the agencies and individuals contributing to the study had a brief for civil liberties and public service concerns for the whole community. Is there a special or separate place in this debate for learning and the education community?

The access constraints outlined earlier apply more widely than in education. The cost, availability, and relevance of electronic knowledge, the awareness of its existence and competence in gaining access to it are criteria which are common to all civic and public service purposes. Learning has, however, its own particular needs and priorities.

The learning process spans such a wide range of activities, institutions and resources that it would be unwise to generalise, for example, about the regulatory conditions most appropriate to a small business manager in a Kent village, a pensioner living alone in a high-rise block on a Hull housing estate and a teenager at a secondary school in Dundee, beyond arguing that they should promote easy, affordable access to the widest range of interactive multimedia learning resources and communications networks available.

This view does not, however, dilute the case to be made for learners' needs in relation to the ISH. It rather strengthens the argument for each group within the education and training community to make itself aware of its electronic learning needs and the means of making sure they are met.

Towards A More Equitable Access to Electronic Learning: Some Suggestions for an Agenda

These suggestions are offered cautiously, in the awareness that effort is already being expended along some of these lines in the UK, elsewhere in Europe and further afield and that similar plans may have already been laid of which the author is unaware.

Confidence in the need to assert them stems, however, from the strength of the difference in policy and practice in these areas (having allowed for cultural differences) between the UK and north America, and from their apparent absence or low position on the agendas of the learning community here.

They are brief statements covering a wide, diverse and complex field. Necessarily brief in a report intended to attract the attention of policy-makers, the suggestions contain the seeds for further, more intensive research and for concerted action on several fronts. It is hoped that both will follow as the need for them is more fully appreciated.

Awareness-raising. An awareness-raising programme should be designed and implemented by national and local government, education and training agencies and providers, professional associations, trades unions, learners' representative organisations and the relevant media to ensure that decision-makers at all levels understand the issues affecting access to learning via ICT and their ability to influence them.

Audits. Institutional, local and regional audits should be carried out of existing and projected (over the next five years) needs and resources in electronic learning, quantifying demand, stimulated where appropriate by public sector incentives and contributing to the process of awareness raising.

Strategies. These audits should be used to develop strategies at those levels designed to maximise the benefits and minimise the cost of ICT-based learning to end users. Although focused on learning, the strategies should be cross-sectoral, especially at regional level, to ensure synergy and congruence between, for example, the objectives of local education authorities, TECs, economic development departments, universities and companies.

Cross-sectoral initiatives. These strategies should be used by potential stakeholders to evaluate the relevance and feasibility of the growing number of initiatives in this area and, where appropriate, to encourage them and direct them towards meeting access-oriented goals.

Consumer power. Learning providers and users should use the information gained through audits and awareness campaigns to negotiate with ICT suppliers on, for example, favourable tariffs and special services for disadvantaged groups, as far as regulation allows.

Campaigns. Organisations representing the interests of learners, educators and disadvantaged groups should take on the responsibility of finding out about their constituents' needs in this area, how these needs are met by suppliers and the regulatory agencies, and, where appropriate, mount campaigns to ensure that they are fairly served.

Public sector pioneers. Those agencies and institutions who have ICT capability should, where appropriate, take a lead in marketing it to public and private sector users in their localities as a means of driving down costs and spreading awareness and competence.

Product/market development. The communications industry at all levels should make full use of cross-sectoral partnerships and opportunities to work with disadvantaged groups and those representing them as a way of developing user-friendly mass and niche market products and of growing markets. Government agencies should consider ways of facilitating these relationships. Industry analysts and managers should focus on the particular management features and information economy conditions, including the intellectual property rights environment which favour profitable indigenous and local production.

Local learning networks. Learning providers at local level should use their audits and strategies to consider ways of developing effective, self-financing local learning networks and materials in cross-sectoral partnerships to ensure that due access is available to the wealth of learning resources at this level and that the infrastructure exists to enable full-scale local communication between learners and teachers.

'Big switches'. Institutional providers, especially in higher and further education, should evaluate the potential of collaborative ICT-based production and distribution systems at regional, national and international levels as a way of reaching non-traditional learners and achieving economies of scale.

The global view. Development agencies should evaluate the role of ICT in the areas with which they are concerned and consider ways in which the expertise available to them conventionally and electronically can be exploited to enhance their work.

The media should continue their move away from an uncritical embrace of the superhighway and its traffic to extend the attention they have begun to focus on questions of equity and social justice in electronic communications.

Government should review the means available to it for promoting these goals through national regulation, in concert with industry and at local and regional level through carefully designed, monitored and evaluated initiatives.

APPENDIX 1

Contributor Profiles

Contributor Profiles by Sector

State/Province Government and Public Sector Agencies

The CUE Fall Conference
Hawaii Inc
Hawaii State Senate
Industry Council for Technology in Learning
Massachusetts Corporation for Educational Telecommunications
Open Learning Agency

Regional Public Sector Agencies

Far West Laboratory
Pacific Region Educational Laboratory
Western Co-operative for Educational Telecommunications

Post School Distance Learning Organisations

The Annenberg/CPB Projects
Distance Education and Training Council
Mind Extension University
National Technological University
University of Phoenix Online Campus

National Campaigning Organisations

Benton Foundation
Center for Media Education
Council of Chief State School Officers

The Communications Industry

Bell Atlantic
Cable in the Classroom
Community Learning and Information Network (CLIN) Inc
The Curriculum Network
Ingenius
Jones International Ltd
Microsoft
Vistar Technologies

Federal Government Departments and Agencies

Congress of the United States Office of Technology Assessment
Federal Communications Commission
US Department of Commerce National Telecommunications and
Information Administration (NTIA)
US Department of Education

International Agencies

The British Council
The Commonwealth of Learning
East-West Center
Pacific Telecommunications Council
PEACESAT

Individual Experts

Professor David J Farber
Rob Glaser
Professor Robert Harris
Dr Meheroo Jussawalla
Dr Catherine Murray

Contributor Profiles

Alphabetical Listing

The Annenberg/CPB Projects

Dr Stephen C Ehrmann
Senior Program Officer for Interactive Technologies

Initiated in 1981, the Project is 'dedicated to helping colleges and universities use technologies to extend and enrich undergraduate education, especially for working adults unable to regularly attend on-campus courses.' The original project was augmented in 1991 by a further one funded at $3.3 million per year by the Annenberg Foundation to support the use of technology to 'accelerate the pace of reform of math and science education in US schools.'

CPB, the Corporation for Public Broadcasting, is a non-profit corporation created by an Act of Congress and funded from federal, foundation and corporate sources to support public telecommunications, mainly public television and public radio, in the US.

The Project's activities include New Pathways to a Degree, a scheme embracing seven diverse, post-school institution-based projects designed to serve students who may not otherwise enrol in or complete a degree course; Perseus, a project to develop software for distribution on the World Wide Web, and a range of initiatives in professional development and evaluation.

Comment

The Project is one of the key initiatives in promoting effective collaborative action among institutions offering continuing education. Its link with the public broadcasting service enable it to undertake software research and development activities in which these institutions have a stake.

Bell Atlantic

C Lincoln Hoewing
Executive Director, External Affairs – Education, Health, Strategic Issues

As the Regional Bell Operating Company (RBOC), for many of the eastern states Bell Atlantic is involved in several initiatives designed to explore the ISH's potential for education and its own role as a provider of interactive services in the new environment. It has concentrated on public schools and libraries rather than higher education which tends to operate its own networks.

These initiatives are typically exploratory partnerships. The examples given were:

- Blackbury, West Virginia where the company has contributed $200,000 to the cost of hardware in a wired city project managed by a non-profit board with the option of becoming profit-based as revenues develop
- Union City, New Jersey where the company worked with the Centre for Educational Technology to design an e-mail-based system to link homes and schools in a home-based learning project whose first year results show improvements in writing and comprehension skills and a decline in truancy.

Comment

Bell offers a good example of positive intervention by the telephone companies in developing local infrastructure, applications and systems in education which explore the long-term role of the technology as well as paying public affairs dividends.

Benton Foundation

Andrew Blau
Director, Communications Policy Project

The Foundation is the legacy of Senator William Benton. It was set up in 1980 to 'encourage the use of the techniques and technologies of communications to advance the democratic process'.

The Project, headed by Andrew Blau, aims to involve non-profit groups in 'shaping the NII [National Information Infrastructure] to promote the public interest'. Its programmes include symposia on universal service policy and on the NII's role in supporting democratic participation in government, a catalogue of electronic, home-delivered education and health care services, research into public sentiment and values on communications issues and the production of print and video materials to stimulate public discussion in the field.

His 1994 testimony to the US Senate Subcommittee on Communications argues that NII regulation must create favourable treatment for non-profits because they are necessary to the realisation of the technology's potential in education, health care, community development, social services, the arts and democratic participation, but cannot compete with the private sector for access on commercial terms. The testimony cites public opinion research conducted for the Foundation showing 'strong public support for the idea of communications companies turning back some portion of their resources for community use to deliver community benefits.'

Comment

Spanning the all-too-frequent gap between formal research and public campaigning, the Project is making an extremely valuable contribution to public debate in the US on the impact of the ISH. Its equivalent in the UK does not exist and is strongly needed.

The British Council

David Evans
Director

David Evans expressed an interest in any follow up to the Fellowship that could help forge on-going relations in this area in the UK.

Cable in the Classroom

Megan Stevens Hookey
Associate Director

This small organisation (a staff of six) was set up five years ago by the US cable industry system operators and programme service providers. Its cost of $1.5 million is met by voluntary membership dues.

Members provide a free cable connection to all schools in their area and make free delivery of programmes to one outlet in the school: more, apparently, in many schools. The scheme, according to Megan Hookey, reaches 65 per cent (35 million students) of the 100,000 K-12 schools in the US.

Programme provider members have said they will air commercial-free educational programmes for 15 minutes a day (or night) on CNN with print and data support delivered by fax or modem. Study guides are also produced. All materials must have copyright clearance so that teachers can tape and keep them for a year. As curricula are determined by each state, members point out appropriate links in their support materials.

CIC produces a magazine with a subscription of 96,000 which acts as a response trigger from teachers. Half the networks have set up education committees, while Megan Hookey and her staff conduct about 120 meetings a year with schools. There are contests and incentives for teachers. In the last survey of a random sample of 1,000 teachers two-thirds had apparently used the service in the previous month.

Comment

Megan Hookey readily points out that the service is seen by its members as good public relations, both to counter hostile response to the cable industry in recent years and to strengthen its position now in relation to the telecom companies and other competitors on the superhighway.

Cable Television Laboratories Inc

Donald P Dulchinos
Senior Analyst

CableLabs was set up in 1988 as a research and development consortium of cable television system operators, now representing over 85 per cent of US, 70 per cent of Canadian and 10 per cent of Mexican subscribers. An annual income of $11 million is based on 2 cents per subscriber per month. Its stated mission is to 'plan and fund research and development projects; transfer technologies to member companies and industry suppliers; serve as a clearing house to provide information on current and prospective technological developments.'

Current priorities include:

- a project on advanced network development from initial signal generation to the TV set, examining, for example, how these networks can deploy high capacity digital and analogue systems, interactive services and multi-channel movies
- co-ordinating the development and implementation of advanced television systems
- working with vendors and consumer electronics manufacturers to implement technologies which will help consumers make better use of future services.

Comment

After rapid expansion in the 1980s the cable industry is now also in competition with Direct Broadcast Satellite (DBS) services, introduced to the US in 1994, and video for entertainment services. Its position on the ISH will be determined by the extent to which it can compete effectively with the telephone companies and computer service providers in the delivery of interactive multimedia services. For this reason the future for the cable industry lies in adding intelligence to its networks through computer technology. In Long Island, for example, the local operator has built its own fibre optic 'ring' allowing regional companies to link their design and production offices for CAD/CAM in a process known as 'agile manufacturing.'

CableLabs plays a key strategic role in this competition.

Center for Media Education

Jeffrey A Chester
Executive Director

Anthony E Wright
Co-ordinator, Future of Media Project

The Center is a non-profit public interest policy and research organisation dedicated to promoting the democratic potential of the electronic media. Launched in 1991 with a $15,000 grant from the **Benton Foundation** by Jeffrey Chester, a social worker turned documentary producer, and his wife, Kathryn Montgomery, an ex-UCLA assistant professor of TV history and criticism, it deliberately achieves wide media coverage for its work. Now funded by foundations to about $500,000, the Center acts as a resource for non-profits in this field.

The Future Media Project, mounted by the Center, is designed to raise awareness of and advocate consumer issues in electronic communications. In 1994 it started a campaign with the Consumer Federation of America, the nation's largest consumer advocacy organisation with some 30 million members, to create a 'consumer highway patrol' for the ISH to safeguard the interests of telephone ratepayers (subscribers) in its construction.

In an attempt to bring organisations together on a continuing basis to stimulate debate in Washington, DC The Center established, also in 1994, The Telecommunications Policy Round Table with its own Internet Discussion List, the Round Table and a membership of 150 groups. Its principles are:

- all people should have affordable access to the information infrastructure
- the information infrastructure should enable all people to effectively exercise their fundamental right to communicate
- the information infrastructure must have a vital civic sector at its core
- the information infrastructure should ensure competition among ideas and information providers
- new technologies should be used to enhance the quality of work and to promote equity in the workplace
- privacy should be carefully protected and extended

- the public should be fully involved in policy making for the information infrastructure.

The Center also publishes *InfoActive*, a monthly newsletter for non-profits.

Comment

The urgency pervading the Center's work is generated by their awareness that there is a small window of opportunity (two years?) to influence crucial, strategic decisions about the ISH which, once taken, will have an enduring and largely unrealised effect.

It is not easy to find a UK or European equivalent, though the need for one is just as great.

The Commonwealth of Learning

Richard J Simpson
Director, Communications Technologies and Information

Dr Abdul W Khan
Senior Program Officer, Educational Technology

COL is an international organisation set up by Commonwealth governments in 1988. Its purpose is to create and widen access to education and to improve its quality through distance learning and communications technology, meeting the particular requirements of member countries.

Its programmes and activities, aimed at strengthening their capacity to develop the human resources needed for economic and social advancement, are carried out in collaboration with governments, universities and colleges and other relevant agencies. Training distance educators is a key function.

The agency has helped set up over 50 teleconferencing units in Commonwealth countries and is promoting the use of computers for interpersonal and inter-institutional networking. It is pioneering a cost-effective regional multimedia materials delivery service.

Aware of the need to achieve economies of scale in buying and using communications technology, especially in small member states, COL is keen to develop multi-user networking. It has been working with the idea of learning centres (like telecottages) shared by institutions. At a strategic level, COL is involved in advocacy with the International Telecommunications Union (ITU), arguing for more collaboration between telecoms and education.

Comment

This relatively small agency has the massive task of addressing, among other things, the electronic learning needs and resources of over 50 culturally, economically and geographically diverse countries. The issues it is addressing around access to learning via communications technology are, however, the same in kind as those dealt with elsewhere in this report.

Community Learning and Information Network (CLIN) Inc

Stanley L Newman
Director, Government Programs

Vince Darago
Vice-President, International

CLIN is a non-profit corporation set up in 1992 with the mission of bringing the ISH to poor schools. The CLIN approach is described as a shared usage model in which educational institutions are helped to set up interactive multimedia community learning centres with local area networks (LANs) connected by satellite links.

This venture sets out to spread the capital and running costs of facilities in local schools by helping them to hire capacity to public and private clients in the area for training and communication. These clients are likely to include the military's programme for training citizen soldiers. One example cited was South Bend, Indiana's public housing university whose facilities are being offered to the local Marriott hotel for training.

CLIN is run by a core staff of six plus consultants. It is understood to have affiliates in 16 states and has set itself the target of 516 sites.

Comment

CLIN is an ambitious venture with a strongly expressed commitment to promoting equality of access to education via electronic communication. It is one version of a range of highly innovative, locally based public/private sector partnership schemes set up to achieve the same goal.

Computer-Using Educators, Inc

CUE is an information giving and advocacy service for Californian educators. It produces a newsletter containing details of policy and practice developments. Its advocacy priorities for 1994/3 include: 'the creation of a governance structure for (the) California educational community which promotes inter-segmental cooperation in the development and use of educational technology resources' and 'require colleges, universities, districts and schools to have technology use plans to receive state technology funding.'

The fall conference and exhibition included 220 sessions, 200 exhibits, professional development seminars and hands-on workshops. It is estimated that about 4,000 teachers, administrators, school board members and other professionals attended. The San Jose University extension offered a semester unit credit to those attending. The California Technology Project's TeleLearning Mobile Unit was on display outside the conference centre. A commercially sponsored trailer containing desktop computers, it offered training and access to interactive services for teachers.

Congress of the United States Office of Technology Assessment

Kathleen L Fulton
Senior Analyst, Project Director

The Office of Technology Assessment, with a staff of 200, carries out studies for Congress in the areas of education and human resources, health, the environment, space and energy. The politically bipartisan Technology Assessment Board oversees these studies to ensure their impartiality. The OTA presents options to Congress rather than making specific recommendations.

Kathleen Fulton is Director of a project with the working title of Teachers in Technology, due for completion in early 1995. Requested in 1993, the study is guided by a 17-person Advisory Committee on which all the stakeholders are represented. Most of the work is carried out by experts in the field on a contract basis. It is concerned with teachers and how communications technology affects them and is exploring the proposition that successful implementation requires not only systems training but also a vision for curriculum development and continuing support. Although the study is focused on K-12 it covers higher education from the point of view of its role in preparing teachers to use educational technology.

As education is organised at state and local, rather than federal level, it is argued that many people in the field look to the OTA for guidance, adding to the study's impact.

Comment

Several key reports on electronic learning have originated in the OTA. Many of the people met during this tour knew of its work and held it in high regard.

Council of Chief State School Officers

Frank B Withrow
Director, Learning Technologies

The Council is a nationwide, non-profit organisation comprised of the department heads of elementary and secondary education in all the states and (in some states) other aspects of education, and other areas of US educational administration.

In addition to representing the chief education administrators and speaking on behalf of the state education agencies the Council undertakes policy- and administration-oriented initiatives and helps federal agencies implement their programmes. Chief state school officers receive twice-weekly electronic briefings on education issues at federal and international levels via CHIEFLINE.

One of these initiatives is the Learning Technologies Program. In support of the Council's commitment to ensuring that all learners have access to ISH services, a report is being prepared recommending ways that federal, state and local governments can develop policies to help teachers and learners achieve the National Education Goals by using National Information Infrastructure resources. This commitment is extended through a network of state technology representatives appointed by chief state school officers to work with the Council in identifying, sharing and assessing new learning technology.

The Council's 1991 policy statement *Improving Student Performance through Learning Technologies* makes these recommendations to its members:

- develop a state plan for the use of technology in education
- ensure that the state, districts and schools have sufficient funding to initiate and sustain on-going use of technology as articulated in the state plan
- ensure that students and school personnel have equitable access to technologies for their learning, teaching and management needs
- ensure that educators have the staff support, training, time, authority, incentive and resources necessary to use technology effectively
- encourage the development and expansion of telecommunications networks
- support the use of technology in student assessment to measure and report accumulated complex accomplishments and new student outcomes
- develop national leadership for learning technologies.

Comment

The Council has a particularly important role to play in orchestrating opinion, innovating and disseminating good policy and practice and lobbying both corporate and government decision makers, given the complex and decentralised nature of educational administration in the US. Its strong emphasis on and clear analysis of policy and resource issues relating to learning technology as long ago as 1991 is some indicator of the vision it brings to this role.

The Curriculum Network

This public/private partnership between **Far West Laboratory**, North Central Regional Educational Laboratory, Pacific Mountain Network (a public broadcasting agency) and Screen Media Partners (a commercial consultancy specialising in the design and launch of large-scale media systems) has been set up to provide middle and high schools with a library of regionalised video-based curriculum support units in core subject areas and a technology planning and leasing programme covering all areas of school activity.

A pilot based on 15 schools was planned in which the equipment and materials tied to the national Education Goals and Goals 2000 would be tested. Its explanatory note states: 'Interested schools will subscribe to the Curriculum Network and receive a library of Curriculum Support Units – seven to ten minute mini-programs combining audio and full motion video, which establish the links between identified curriculum areas and real-world reference points. The curriculum content can be customised for individual regions ... In-depth training will be included.' The Network is intended to be financed by subscription, to include technology leasing costs, and by public/private sector underwriting.

Comment

Although in its early stages at the time of interview, the project's public sector support and curriculum-driven approach add to its potential.

Distance Education and Training Council

Michael P Lambert
Executive Director

The DETC claims that there are about two and a half million distance education students in the US, representing a $3.5 billion per year business. A membership organisation, its main functions are accreditation and publishing.

Its main target market is 25–35-year-olds in their first career who are dissatisfied and want to move. 'Third-agers' are also an important group for the Council's members: 60 per cent of one school's enrolment is over 60 years old.

The DETC sees its commercial strength in identifying 'niche courses' which the universities do not have the time or money to develop. A typical DETC member course costs $700 and costs $1 million to develop. To recoup this level of investment great emphasis is placed on market research and only courses which have perceived benefits to buyers are offered. Recruitment is through direct marketing using specialist magazine advertisements, cable TV commercials with toll-free numbers and telephone solicitation. Although DETC are to an extent in competition with the public universities, Michael Lambert can see them making approaches for partnership ventures.

The vast bulk of the Council's work is print-based but they are increasingly using computers and bulletin boards for on-line learning. Multimedia courses are so far mainly in electronics-based disciplines. The DETC offers a Master's degree in information management. Its policy is to respond rather than lead in the introduction of new learning technology.

Comment

Although commercially driven, the DETC's customer-facing approach has lessons for more conventional, top-down educational provision. In keeping with this approach, they emphasise 'raw lesson completion rate' (an average 65 per cent of student/lessons completed) rather than the rate of graduation, arguing that graduation may not be the prime goal for career changing or leisure-oriented students who will follow a course until it has met their needs.

The DETC, under its former name, the National Home Study Council, started in 1926. Distance education has a long history in the US due partly, as with mail order, to the history of settlement in which geographical isolation is often combined with geographical and social mobility.

Professor David J Farber

Alfred Fitler Moore Professor of Telecommunications Systems, University of Pennsylvania

Professor Farber started the Computer Science Network, one of the early components of the Internet. He now advises on policy in this field at national level and is widely regarded as one of the most eminent strategic thinkers in this field.

Comment

The conversation with Professor Farber covered, among other topics, Internet funding and ISH regulation. He was concerned at the fate of people in the inner city who would suffer an increased knowledge gap unless a way was found of taking IT to them. Libraries, he argued had a key role in this process. Having lost their ground since the days when Benjamin Franklin founded the free library in Philadelphia they can be returned to the centre of activity, reframed as information specialists.

Far West Laboratory

John Cradler
Director, Educational Technology

The FWL's mission is 'to challenge and enable educational organisations and their communities to create and sustain improved learning and development opportunities for their children, youth and adults.'

Founded in 1966, it is one of 20 regional educational laboratories around the US set up to conduct research and development in order to improve education. It now employs 153 people on an annual programme funding budget of $17.5 million. $4.3 million of this comes from the US Department of Education, the remainder is specific project funding from the same department, the US Department of Health and Human Services, the National Science Foundation, the California State Department of Education, the Arizona Department of Education, universities, school districts, foundations and other state and local agencies.

FWL has carried out over 400 projects covering research into policy and practice, development of products and programmes for teachers and learners, linking agencies and institutions and providing a forum for discussion among educators. Its educational technology initiative consists of 11 programmes designed to:

- 'facilitate access to and dissemination of exemplary technology- based learning resources to educational agencies and organisations that assist the school level adoption and adaptation of these services
- provide and make available support services to assist the planning, development, implementation and evaluation of

educational technology programs and projects at the
school, district, regional, state and national level
- facilitate and inform the development of regional, state and
national policy for educational technology
- establish partnerships with professional education agencies
and businesses that result in the development of resources
to support the strategic objectives of FWL and the agencies
it serves.'

John Cradler was one of the two principal authors of *The National Information Infrastructure: Requirements for education and training*, prepared by the National Coordinating Committee on Technology in Education and Training in March 1994.

Comment

FWL plays a leading role in promoting electronic learning across its region at all levels from helping formulate state policy to evaluating good practice in the classroom. John Cradler's involvement in federal policy-making means that he is one of the leading national figures in this area. The composition of its funding base adds to FWL's entrepreneurialism.

Federal Communications Commission

Donald H Gips
Deputy Chief, Office of Plans and Policy

The FCC regulates cable television, satellite and terrestrial broadcasting and communications, telegraphy, telephony and two-way radio at interstate and international levels. The Commission itself is composed of five members appointed by the President. They are assisted by a General Council and a staff organised in offices and bureaux whose remits include cable services, common carriers, engineering and technology, legislative affairs, mass media and plans and policy.

It develops and recommends policy in these and other areas, conducts research, allocates frequencies, issues licences, oversees the effective and responsible operation of services through a network of field offices, deals with state authorities, and investigates complaints and enquiries from the public.

The FCC was established in 1934, since when no radical change in electronic communications regulation at federal level had taken place in the US. As the federal agency with a brief extending across all the elements of the ISH, the FCC's role in its creation is potentially great. The legislation determining its actual contribution is yet to be passed.

Comment

Electronic learning has not previously been an area of FCC responsibility but it has now decided to 'bully pulpit,' bringing moral pressure to bear on the CTV and telecoms providers to make realistic provision for educational institutions. At a strategic level it is also concerned that the pattern of regulatory incentives over which it presides does not steer people towards the wrong technology. Schools, for example, are investing in local area networks (LANs). It is concerned more particularly with K-12 rather than higher education. There is an awareness that the cost of effectively linking the K-12 sector to the ISH is more than anyone is prepared to spend. As the relative cost-effectiveness of electronic learning has been demonstrated through experiment, regulatory questions cluster around the right level of incentive needed to change the risk paradigm so that investment takes place. Options for the Administration include 'jump starting' either the product market or the connectivity market.

The FCC's capacity to intervene in education, as in other areas, was at the time of the interview very much dependent on the outcome of the Telecommunications Bill, though the intention was, in any case, to work more closely with the individual states. The Bill would, for example, have required the FCC to explore ways of setting preferential rates for schools, libraries and healthcare. The forthcoming congressional elections were expected to affect the ways of working to achieve change, though the principle of putting education on the ISH is apparently bipartisan.

Rob Glaser

President and Chief Executive Officer, Progressive Networks

Rob Glaser is a multimedia specialist who is active in lobbying for the socially responsible development of the ISH. An ex-Microsoft executive, he now runs Progressive Networks, a company which creates technology to link learning to consumption and is developing a network of commercial and non-profit people and materials to extend the use of the ISH for social education.

He is also a key figure in the Electronic Frontier Foundation, founded to raise public consciousness of cyberspace as a community to which the civil liberties and rights of the physical community should be extended.

Comment

Rob Glaser's industry background enables him to speak with authority on the civic and social dimensions of the ISH. His insight into the 'platform debate' (the struggle for dominance of the ISH by the cable, computer and telecoms industries) was especially helpful.

Professor Robert G Harris

Principal, Law and Economics Consulting Group Inc

Robert Harris is an Associate Professor in the Walter A Haas School of Business at the University of California, Berkeley, specialising in regulatory economics and telecommunications policy. He has carried out research into the effects of economic regulation and anti-trust policy on economic performance and the implications of changing technologies and economics for public policy in telecoms and related topics. He has been a consultant to, among others, the US Office of Technology Assessment, the US Department of Justice, the California Department of Consumer Affairs and several major telecoms companies. At the time of the interview he was a member of a task-force advising on telecoms in California.

Comment

Professor Harris saw the ISH's role in higher education as a necessary means of increasing cost effectiveness by delivering high quality teaching to a larger student base. His views on the danger of uninformed regulation were a valuable counter to the easily reached position that statutory intervention is the automatic solution to access problems.

Hawaii INC

Arthur F Koga
Director

Set up in 1991 with funding from Hawaii State, Hawaii Information Network Corporation is a gateway for the public to about 90, mainly public, services available on-line via a (free) local call, similar to the French Minitel system.

Services include database access as support for broadcast distance learning, consumer information, careers and business guidance, including access to a legal database and connectivity to mainland universities.

About 7,000 people have registered to use the service, yielding 170,000 accesses per month. It is likely, however, that many more use it, as registration is not necessary for some of the services.

Some fee-paying services have been offered but these have not yet attracted as much revenue as expected.

Comment

Hawaii INC is one of a growing number of public access-oriented on-line facilities emerging from the state's strategic approach to the technology and helping to create a rich electronic communications environment in the public service.

Hawaii State Senate

Senator Carol Fukunaga
Chair, Legislative Management, Hawaii State Senate and Member of the National Information Infrastructure Advisory Council

Two thousand miles west of mainland USA, spread over seven islands whose communities are further separated by mountains, the state of Hawaii could be said to have major communication problems. It is perhaps for this reason that the state government responded early to the ISH's potential and is developing a wide area integrated information network system. Work started in 1986 but the pace is quickening as the need emerges for more creativity in, for example, taking advantage of partnership and information sharing opportunities and developing better models. An intersectoral approach to infrastructure planning is not a problem because Hawaii is a small state.

It is now embarked on an education project intended to be the biggest public sector deployment in the US. The Hawaii Research and Education Network (Hawaiian name: *Ala Ike*, the knowledge way/path) has been launched as a three-year pilot project funded by the National Science Foundation designed to meet the State Department of Education's commitment to create: 'appropriate access to voice, data and video information systems for every public school student, teacher and administrator regardless of their location or learning environment by the year 2000.'

The project will use the Internet to link the Department's 180,000 K-12 students, 110,000 adult learners and 17,000 staff in 300 sites on the seven islands with the University of Hawaii's 50,000 students and 7,500 staff on nine campuses over six islands and the East-West Center's 1,500 graduate students and 800 faculty on one site plus locations across the region with state-wide network resources including a supercomputer on the island of Maui. It will explore use of the network for learning, research and administration.

While this system is being implemented the Department is also decentralising the school system. Education is a priority for Hawaii, accounting for 60 per cent (about $700 million) of the state budget. An analysis of potential educational technology costs suggests an expenditure of about $50 million a year over the next five years.

Although development costs are high it is argued that there is a need to gain support for them by educating the population to see that the cost of not building an infrastructure will be rising crime levels, low growth and a shrinking tax base resulting from companies leaving the islands and a failure to compete globally. Communications technology itself is used in this process by inviting the public into the planning process using, for example, access programming on cable television. The small, participatory, local cable systems have themselves emerged partly as a product of Hawaii's topography and partly through state regulatory pressure on the system operators.

Comment

It may be argued that, like Singapore's, Hawaii's circumstances make its infrastructure unique. This should not detract, however, from its importance as a model for integrated infrastructure planning and development. Experience in Hawaii and elsewhere suggests that island politics are fertile breeding grounds for integrated infrastructure development. This may be owing to a mixture of strong, coherent, cultural identity and a manageable administrative scale but calls for further investigation.The islands have long played a strategic role in the Pacific, reflected now in their participation in the region's wider ISH plans.

Senator Fukunaga's contribution to this area is recognised in her membership of the National Information Infrastructure Council.

Industry Council for Technology in Learning

Rick Larkey
Executive Director

The ICTL is a non-profit corporation set up in 1992 as an initiative of the Industry Education Council of California. Its mission is to improve lifelong learning opportunities in California by:

- collaboratively moving the state in a clear, concerted direction for educational technologies
- working with groups such as the Education Council for Technology in Learning to implement the California Master Plan for Educational Technology
- making policy and legislative recommendations based on a common technological approach
- developing projects and relationships to expedite the mission.

The ICTL draws its members from business, education, foundations, government and non-profit organisations in California. Its plans include a Learning Technology Institute with the potential of reaching 6,000 education leaders, local initiatives to connect schools to the ISH and an on-line service giving access to information on educational technology projects and funding sources.

Comment

The author attended a one-day conference organised by the ICTL where speakers included Dindo Rivera, Western States President of IBM, and Michael Powell from Pacific Bell. The conference drew attention to the need for education to succeed in retaining students, to deliver a workforce capable of reversing relative economic decline in the state and to help offset social inequalities.

Ingenius

Dr Gerald E Bennington
Chief Executive Officer

Ingenius is a joint venture between TCI, the major US cable operator, and Reuters, set up to deliver interactive multimedia learning products via cable to homes and schools. Its first product, *What on Earth*, is a daily report of global events compiled by a 20-strong production team of educators, journalists and multimedia designers who select six stories a day and compile video, audio and text coverage of them from the news media. The package is to be downloaded via cable into standard multimedia computers in homes and schools. Designed to be used at different skill levels in varying curriculum areas directly by students, it incorporates guidance for teachers and exercises.

The product had not been launched at the time of the visit though it was intended to be available in the US shortly afterwards at a subscription of between $100 and $200 a year. It is developed from X.CHANGE, an educational service delivering text news and information from over 20 international information providers and wire services.

Comment

The service raises important questions about the role of the ISH in changing learning and teaching practice by delivering an abundance of stimulating, student-user-friendly resources directly to home and school, and about the impact of these materials on curriculum content. What role, for example, should the teacher play in an environment where attractive learning materials are no longer a scarce resource, are designed to be used directly by students in and out of the classroom and whose content is shaped by a journalistic paradigm similar to that prevailing in broadcasting and newspapers?

Jones International Ltd

James N Ginsburg
Senior Information Officer, Jones Interactive Inc

Adrienne E Thiele
Vice President, Promotional Media, Jones Education Networks

Adam Dempsey
Director of Affiliate Relations, Special Markets

Jones International is the corporate parent of 17 subsidiaries in the communications (mainly cable) industry. Glenn R Jones, its founder, chairman and President, has a strong commitment to popular education which is reflected in the subsidiaries' activities. Jones Education Networks, Inc runs several companies delivering lifelong learning to broad-based audiences.

Mind Extension University (ME/U), the first of these to start, maintains a 24-hour satellite delivered television network offering eight undergraduate and graduate credit bearing courses; professional workforce development courses; language, computer skills, information literacy and personal enrichment courses.

The network reaches about 26 million US TV households. About 20 per cent of its output is made in-house, the rest by the more than 30 affiliated colleges and universities contributing to the network. ME/U is developing partnerships to set up campuses in Africa, Asia, Europe and South America.

Launched in 1993, the Jones Computer Network carries 28 hours a week of programming on IT-related themes including news and magazine shows about the industry, 'how to' and degree/certificate programmes.

Jones Interactive, Inc develops digital publishing and interactive multimedia projects.

Comment

Jones' commitment to broad-based learning has led to initiatives in targeting disadvantaged groups. Available in a high proportion of the cities with substantial African-American and Hispanic populations, ME/U Special Markets is developing local community and industry support to make the service available to these groups who are reached through carefully targeted publicity. It has funded scholarships for minorities to study via the network.

Dr Meheroo F Jussawalla

Senior Fellow/Economist, Program on Communications and Journalism, East-West Center

An internationally prominent figure in this field, Dr Jussawalla's interest lies in telecoms regulatory policy, especially in relation to investment and markets. She has written widely on this topic and on the economics of communication at both Asia-Pacific and global level.

Comment

The economics of information and of the communications technology carrying it is the most significant yet least widely appreciated set of factors influencing access to learning. Dr Jussawalla's work in this field and in the related area of telecoms regulatory policy in the Pacific region and at global level is a major contribution to an understanding of this field.

Massachusetts Corporation for Educational Telecommunications

Dr John G Flores
Executive Director

Irwin Hipsman
Network Facilities Marketing Manager

Chris Viegaard
Program Services Co-ordinator

MCET is a quasi-autonomous public corporation of the Common-wealth of Massachusetts, receiving about half its funding ($5.5 million) from the state. The balance comes from corporate, federal and foundation grants, including $2.3 million from the Star Schools Programme.

Its mission is 'To take leadership in telecommunications-based education by altering the relationship between people and learn-ing from passive to interactive by providing responsive, cost-effec-tive, innovative programs that utilise multiple technologies.'

Eighty-five per cent of Massachusetts' 350 school districts are MCET members. A $2,000 fee gives schools a VCR, TV monitor and a satellite receiving dish. Subscribers to the nationally avail-able, satellite delivered service from 37 other states pay more.

Its main service is the Mass LearnPike, delivering one-way video, two-way audio programming, supported by print curriculum ma-terials to K-12 schools from its own studios. The Mass LearnNet offers a gateway to the Internet and e-mail facilities. Response to programming is either by telephone or e-mail. It had 3,800 e-mail users by the end of 1993. MCET also operates a video conference unit, available for hire to other public sector users in the state and is supporting the development of interactive videodisc pro-grammes and a CTV/telematics-based integrated learning system.

Programming is made in association with educators from schools, colleges and universities nationwide and in funding partnerships with private companies, including Nynex and Apple.

Comment

MCET is an interesting model of a public sector, plurally-funded venture in electronic learning. Its success in attracting funds as an electronic learning provider is now allowing it to secure its base by diversifying into the provision of electronic communications services for other public sector agencies. In this role as a develop-ment node for ISH services it is helping to educate the wider com-munity in their use.

Microsoft

Tom Corddry
Creative Director, Consumer Division

Microsoft is the world's largest software company: over 80 per cent of all PCs are sold with its software installed. It is developing a position on the ISH through its Microsoft Network on-line service and through strategic alliances with other communication industry companies, with the goal of creating an operating system to control a wide variety of applications available on it.

Microsoft is considering its position *vis-à-vis* the education market. US institutional education, it estimates, spends $400 billion a year. Its deliberations are influenced by the awareness that a 1 per cent share of this expenditure would be roughly equivalent to the company's current yearly profit. The sector, it is argued, is in a similar position to business in 1980, before PCs transformed the role of IT and, in many ways, the structure of company management and the way in which business was done.

A key question for Microsoft planners is: what value can computers add to learning? The wider use of existing technology may add value incrementally but it is also possible that widespread computing may change the learning model over a 20-year timescale.

Comment

The potential role of Microsoft and other major communications companies in shaping the future of education can best be appreciated by the awareness that it is able to bring substantial expertise to bear on a planning horizon of 20 years at global level in contrast with much public sector planning which is, of necessity, local, short-term and reactive.

The company's success so far has resulted from an approach to the market based on 'the paradigm of the person buying value using value.' This approach cuts through the administrative and institutional structures which usually mediate change in education and spans the largely undeveloped market for home-based learning. Factors like these are fundamentally important to strategic planning in which the contribution of hard- and software providers is sometimes seen merely as a matter for consumer choice at implementation stage.

Dr Catherine Murray

Director, Centre for Policy Research on Science and Technology, Simon Fraser University

Catherine Murray has a background in public policy on broadcasting and market research into cable and telecoms. She teaches telecoms regulation and policy.

She is involved in setting up the Canadian Network on Trade, Innovation, Competitiveness and Sustainability (TICS), one of three SFU proposals (another being for a TeleLearning Research Network – see Open Learning Agency below) submitted under the Canadian Networks of Centres of Excellence Program.

Based on existing American, Canadian and Mexican scholarly networks, TICS is designed 'to integrate differing professional perspectives and methods of measuring and evaluating trade, competitiveness and sustainability under the framework of innovation systems in the context of economic and ecological imperatives.'

Comment

The work of Dr Murray and her colleagues has to be seen in the wider context of Canada's version of the US ISH policy formation programme. At the time of the visit the Canadian Radio, Television and Telecommunications Commission (CRTC) had just announced a public hearing process on the ISH, to complement the work of the Government-created Information Highway Advisory Council. This consultation process is intended to inform the Government's strategy in this area which has the objectives of creating jobs through innovation and investment, reinforcing Canadian sovereignty and cultural identity, and ensuring universal access at affordable cost.

The Canadian ISH framework is impressive not only in its coherence but also to the extent that it takes into account Canada's relations with the rest of the world, notably Europe and the other Americas, now linked for trade. A key element in the strategy, as in all Canada's cultural planning and activity, is the need to retain an identity and a domestic industry distinct from that of its southern neighbour.

National Technological University

Dr Gearold R Johnson
Academic Vice-President

The NTU is a private, non-profit, accredited institution delivering postgraduate engineering courses to students in the workplace. Sometimes described as 'a big switch,' it delivers instructional television courses by satellite, uplinked to it from 46 contributing engineering universities in the US, to over 100,000 (1993 figures) enrolled students at 640 sites. Last year it awarded 189 Master's degrees.

Any university can join the NTU system. In 1992/3 it beamed over 22,000 hours of academic credit instruction and 3,000 hours of advanced technology and management programming to its students, 80 per cent of whom time-shifted the material on VCRs. The average class size is eight students, though 27 classes function with only one student.

The programming is supported by print, teleconferencing, e-mail and telephony for tutorials and counselling. Because the average shelf- life of courses is six months, investment in interactive multimedia materials is unrealistic, though HDTV is attractive because of the better resolution it offers. Staff are all retained on contract. All courses are evaluated and the lowest scoring 20 per cent of faculty are replaced each year.

NTU's main target markets are technology, healthcare and law. Its courses are available by satellite in Canada, the US and Mexico, though individual students in other parts of the world receive videos by post. There are advanced plans to expand into Africa, Asia-Pacific (Malaysia, Singapore and pan-regional), Europe and South America.

Comment

The 'big switch' image is strengthened by the physical size of the NTU site. All the administrative, support, teaching and technological operations are run from a small, two-storey office block with a modest dish farm on the outskirts of Fort Collins.

The university's success is due in part to its pricing policy. NTU charges employers $15,000, compared with the $6,000 charge for a conventional university course. NTU's cost compares favourably, however, because employers find it more cost-effective than releasing students who are typically earning $40–50,000. Affiliated universities also benefit, as NTU pays them $9,000.

NTU is one of several institutions in the US whose success depends on targeting niche student markets.

Open Learning Agency

Bodhan Zajcew
Director, Broadcast Policy and Television Program Services

The OLA provides a range of services to learners mainly in British Columbia and the North West Territories. Its principal output, the Knowledge Network, delivered via cable and satellite to over 400,000 viewers a week across the full learning spectrum, carries more than 5,000 hours of television programming a year, of which 166 hours are produced internally and 60 per cent is Canadian in content.

Programme areas include arts and humanities, career and personal development, economic development, the environment, health, lifestyles, science and technology social and political issues.

The Agency has also developed initiatives in open learning which include specially adapted computers and courses for disabled people; a basic skills laboratory in which an adult-oriented flexible programming model combining computer-based training and open learning materials with instructional support is being developed for extension across the province; dial-in electronic learning services for remote areas; courses delivered through First Nations learning centres; vocational training courses and an Educational Credit Bank.

OLA is also contributing to the federal government's TeleLearning Network of Centres of Excellence initiative (see **Dr Catherine Murray**). This private/public funded venture has as its main goal the development of telelearning's effectiveness as an environment that is as good as or better than traditional classrooms for learning. Research carried out under its aegis will cover: the design of learning and technical systems; new approaches to extending access to learning resources in homes and institutions; the economic, social and policy implications of telelearning for governments, industry and educational organisations in a knowledge based economy.

Seventy per cent of the OLA's (approximately) $C50 million funding comes from the provincial government's Ministry of Skills, Training and Labour, 25 per cent from endowments, special project grants, corporate sponsorship (of its television programmes) and $C1.3 million from its 25,000-strong 'partners in knowledge' supporter network.

Comment

The OLA is fortunate in having a broad reach across the full range of electronic learning applications and systems on a scale which allows effective participation. As a result it is able to pioneer significant developments with a much wider relevance. It is also, like many other agencies whose traditional activity has been educational television, navigating the transition into a multimedia environment with all the policy and resource implications of that change.

Pacific Region Educational Laboratory

John W Kofel
Executive Director

PREL is a non-profit corporation serving not only the State of Hawaii but also the wider Pacific community, including American Samoa, the Northern Mariana Islands, Micronesia, the Marshall Islands and Palau.

Funded by federal and local contracts and grants, PREL is governed by a board representing education administration in each of these entities, as well as parents, teachers, business and government. Its work includes strategic planning, policy development, teacher training, curriculum development, research and providing access to learning through ICT.

A link with **PEACESAT** is enabling them to deliver the Internet to schools free of charge. Under a Star Schools-funded partnership with an educational services district in Spokane, Washington the district is providing IDEANET, a TV and computer network for schools delivering live, interactive instruction in languages, maths, science, the arts and humanities via a satellite whose footprint covers Hawaii.

PREL is also in partnership with the Ohau Wireless Cable Company to provide educational microwave transmission to local schools. The company invests in the hardware, is licensed by that act as an educational provider, buys back 80 per cent of the airtime and sells it commercially. PREL acquires the programming and sells it to the company.

Comment

PREL is the only laboratory whose remit extends beyond US territory. This and the operational flexibility resulting from its independence allow it to innovate on a broad front in a region which is educationally and economically disadvantaged. Remote teacher training is a priority. They are also hoping to improve vocational skills in the region using the technology.

Pacific Telecommunications Council

Richard J Barber
Executive Director

The Council is an international telecommunications organisation acting as a forum for service providers and users, as well as policy-makers and researchers. About half its membership is corporate, a quarter academic and a quarter from government. In addition to its annual conference, the PTC runs seminars, training workshops and undertakes research. Both the US Distance Learning Association and the Asian Association of Open Universities meet at its conference.

Comment

Richard Barber is concerned that the Pacific islands will be left out of the global information society and is actively promoting their interests through conferences. The separate island states spread across the Pacific suffer from a lack of cohesion in addressing common issues. There is a risk that these communities will be bypassed by the telecoms infrastructure developments linking the major economic powers surrounding them.

PEACESAT

Dr Norman Okamura
Associate Specialist in Telecommunications, Social Science Research Institute

Originally established in 1971, the Pan-Pacific Education and Communication Experiments by Satellite (PEACESAT) is a programme of the **US Department of Commerce National Telecommunication and Information Administration.** Its mission is 'to support international distance education, research, telemedicine, emergency management, economic development experiments and applications and to provide an experimental laboratory for research in the development and application of low-cost, narrow band communication technologies.'

Based on the University of Hawaii campus in Honolulu, it offers Internet access and distance learning services based on voice, data and compressed video. It has recently been funded to set up a digital network hubbed in Honolulu. Increased capacity has been based on evidence of user need drawn from NTIA and PEACESAT studies. Its network covers a population of 41 million people in 22 countries with an average per capita income of $4,000 a year.

Comment

The network has established itself as a key element in the region's public service communications infrastructure. It is a good example of the way in which the technology can act as a catalyst for cross-sectoral collaboration in an area whose communities are separated from each other and from the major economic centres by vast tracts of ocean.

TCI (Telecommunications Inc) – J C Sparkman Center for Educational Technology

John R Kuglin
Director

TCI is one of the largest cable operators in the US. It also has substantial investment in UK cable. 16,000 K-12 schools are linked to TCI systems across the US, making its educative programming available to nearly half a million teachers and eight million students.

The output includes the Arts & Entertainment Network, Black Entertainment Television (including the BET on Learning resource), C-Span (political coverage), The Discovery Channel and X.Press X.Change, a news and topical information service also providing cross-curricular lesson plans and a daily educational programming guide.

Located near TCI's headquarters in Denver, the Center has 24 interactive multimedia work stations in a classroom where teachers, school board members, administrators, parents and students from all over the country receive free, hands-on training from its staff in the use of computer and CD ROM applications, networked video, multimedia development, desktop videoconferencing, on-line data services via the Internet and home–school connectivity. Courses are tailor-made to applicants' requirements. TCI also runs occasional satellite delivered in-service teacher training sessions. The Center features resources and applications found successful in the seven TCI supported Showcase/Laboratory Schools around the country.

Comment

The Center offers an impressive service to educators and is an important example of the active role it is possible for a communications company to play in implementing the effective use of the technology by which it earns its living.

US Department of Commerce National Telecommunications and Information Administration (NTIA)

Laura Breeden
Director, The Telecommunications and Information Infrastructure Assistance Program

A key part of the Administration's National Information Infrastructure initiative, the Program provides 50 per cent matching grants to state and local governments, non-profit healthcare providers, school districts, libraries, universities and other non-profit entities. The first grants, a total of about £43 million, were awarded in October 1994. At the time of the interview the Administration had requested a further £66 million for fiscal Year 1995 and £100 million for fiscal year 1996.

The National Information Infrastructure's agenda is to:

- 'promote private sector investment
- extend the "universal service" concept
- promote seamless, interactive, user-driven applications
- ensure information security and network reliability
- improve management of the radio frequency spectrum
- protect intellectual property rights
- co-ordinate with other levels of government (national and international)
- provide access to government information.'

Within this context the Program's goals are to provide funds for planning and demonstration projects to:

- 'promote the development and widespread availability of advanced telecommunications technologies
- enhance the delivery of social services and generally serve the public interest
- promote access to government information and increase civic participation
- support the development of an advanced nationwide telecommunication and information infrastructure.'

Comment

The Program represents a commitment at federal level to developing local, cross-sectoral approaches to access and participation goals. It addresses the need to create incentives for infrastructure provision in economically unattractive areas. In an attempt to find solutions to what is sometimes called 'the last mile problem', the Program's criteria require applicants to set up partnerships using local, non-federal funds.

This first phase of initiatives is being evaluated by a specially designed system to identify the most appropriate local public/private sector models to promote and support the longer term evolution of the ISH. Strategies involving the telecommunications companies will be applied at this stage.

US Department of Education

Dr Linda G Roberts
Special Adviser on Technology

Early in 1994 Congress passed Goals 2000, an education act which set out eight national goals and established for the first time a voluntary set of national standards in core academic areas. The Act calls for planning in educational technology, educational technology as a vehicle for delivering these goals and makes provision for small pump-priming grants to states from the Department.

An initial overall budget of $85 million was being allocated to states at the time of the visit. This expenditure has to be seen in the context of individual state initiatives: Florida, for example, committed in 1993 $55 million over three years for classroom technology and connectivity while Utah had committed $45 million between 1990 and 1994. The Department has also supported local action via its Star Schools program, which focuses on distance learning.

Richard R Riley, the US Secretary of Education, emphasised the importance of electronic learning in his testimony to the US Senate on the Telecommunications Act in May 1994. He also stressed the need to ensure that the NII was not late in reaching low income neighbourhoods where the majority of school children, including African-Americans, Asians, Hispanics and new immigrants, lived.

Within the multi-tiered, locally-based administration of education in the US, the Department can intervene in several ways by:

- producing a national vision linked to states, local communities and the private sector
- influencing FCC policy making towards free ISH access for schools
- funding new ideas in the field
- looking at ways of leveraging the use of the technology in other areas.

The Office of Educational Technology has been established in the Department of Education and has, among other things, carried out an assessment of the technology models and costs associated with connecting K-12 schools to the NII.

Comment

Recently appointed to the Department of Education, Linda Roberts is one of the most prominent figures in electronic learning in the US. Pioneering work in her previous appointment at the Congress of the United States Office of Technology Assessment included directing the projects resulting in the key reports on US electronic learning, *Power On!*, *Linking to Learning* and *Adult Literacy and New Technologies*.

Although the Department's capacity to intervene substantially in provision on the ground is limited, like that of all federal departments and agencies, by the decentralised distribution of power and resources in US government, its central role in NII policy formation indicates the importance attached to education by the Administration in this field.

University of Phoenix

Terri Hedegaard
Vice-President, Online Programs

The University is an incorporated, for profit (though the profits are fed back and there are no shareholders), regionally accredited institution. Its Online degree programmes in business and management run in parallel with the work of its 30 conventional campuses.

Its target student group is working adults (aged 23-plus) learning at home across the US. They number about 1,000. Three-quarters of them have their tuition fees paid by their employers, but some students are eligible for support. Online fees are higher than those for the university's conventional students. While overall costs are comparable, this reflects the smaller on-line class sizes.

Eighty per cent of students are male, reflecting the profile of Compuserve's membership – the main recruitment vehicle. Attempts have been made to recruit more women. This group is, on average, 10 years older and about $14,000 a year richer than the university's other students. In the US, according to Terri Hedegaard, half of all college-enrolled students are adults.

Students dial into the host computer to connect with their learning group. Experiments with audioconferencing are being conducted.

The system is open to all hardware. Lectures, seminars and assignments are conducted by e-mail. The case is made that the non-real time seminars offer more time to reflect on contributions and allow more participation by students who do not perform well in face-to-face encounters. Before-and-after exams measure cognitive gains. The results are similar to those for the university's conventional students. Those on-line spend an average of £12 a month on telephone charges.

Teaching is carried out by about 100 regular part-time faculty, who are contracted on a course by course basis after a three-month assessment and training period. Pay is comparable with conventional teaching.

The Program is expanding and there are plans to offer it in Europe.

Comment

As with ME/U (**Jones International**) and **NTU**, the operation's sheer compactness is impressive. Terri Hedegaard made it clear that the Program is not run for the sake of economy but to meet the needs of a niche market. She argues that it is more cost-effective to set up a dedicated distance teaching programme rather than bolt the approach on to existing services. Computer competence is expected from enrolling students who are not trained in the system's use.

Vistar Technologies

Dr Keith Larick
President

This company has developed managing software to allow the individual use of multimedia learning materials to be monitored centrally in a system. It is the basis of a community learning utility. This concept, originated by Jack Taub, the founder of Compuserve, allows electronic information for learning and other purposes to be treated like electricity or gas: the means of generating and distributing it are centrally owned and managed while individuals pay *pro rata* for its use.

The approach is designed to lower the user cost, allowing access to electronic communication by poorer people while encouraging the publishers of electronic information and learning materials into the market by providing a means of monitoring revenue from their use.

Vistar, it is understood, is contracted to provide this software to Global Digital Utility, a company set up to service local, non-profit utilities. These are being promoted in the US and worldwide, especially in poorer countries like China. International distribution is intended to be via a chain of low power satellites launched by a non-profit enterprise called VITA.

Comment

This extremely innovative approach to a basic access issue, user cost, is still at a pioneering stage but should be watched with close interest.

Western Cooperative for Educational Telecommunications (WCET)

Sally M Johnstone
Director

A programme of the Western Interstate Commission for Higher Education, WCET was set up in 1989 to facilitate resource- and information-sharing in the use of ICT for education. Funded over 50 per cent from membership fees, it represents over 150 universities, colleges, and public agencies from 18 states, as well as private corporations nationwide.

It acts as a clearing house for information and contacts, a planner and facilitator of multi-state projects, an avenue of communication with campus, state and federal policy-makers, a provider of support services and an evaluator/researcher on educational uses of the technology.

Its advocacy contributed to the appointment of an educational representative on a recently formed Federal Communications Commission advisory committee.

Other areas include loans for distance education students, relations with teaching unions and fostering collaboration rather than competition among its members.

A recent audio conference programme focused on such questions as: 'What is your vision for a state-level information infrastructure and how does it fit with your state's existing funding and program priorities?' and 'What state-level planning, financing and decision-making structures will best stimulate and support technological innovations and efficiencies in higher education?'

Comment

WCET appeared as a highly effective interface between planners and practitioners at all levels and, as such, an important model for implementing ICT in higher education.

APPENDIX 2

Documents

Listed below are the details of documents, other than prospectuses and publicity, received from contributors and held by the author.

Adult Literacy and New Technologies, Congress of the United States Office of Technology Assessment 1993

ADEC (Alliance for Distance Learning in California) Summit Executive Summary

A Bill for An Act Relating to Education, Hawaii State Legislature 1994

Blau, A *Testimony before the United States Senate Subcommittee on Telecommunications,* The Benton Foundation

Bossert, P J *Forging New Links: Developing Virtual Learning Environments,* Hawaii State Department of Education Office of Information Technology 1994

Breedon, L *The Telecommunications and Information Infrastructure Assistance Program,* United States Department of Commerce (summary)

Browning, J 'Universal Service: An Idea Whose Time is Past', *Wired,* September 1994

Cable in the Classroom (periodical) October 1994

California State Legislature SB 600 Task Force on Telecommunications Network Infrastructure Subcommittee, *Report on Needs Assessment Grant Program Criteria*

California State Legislature Financing Subcommittee, *Report on the Financing of California's Telecommunications and Information Infrastructure for Schools and Libraries* 1994

California State Legislature SB 600 *Grant Program Criteria Needs Assessment Subcommittee Report*

The California Master Plan for Educational Technology, The California Planning Commission for Educational Technology 1992

Ciciora, W S *An Overview of Cable Television in the United States*, Cable Television Labs 1994

CLIN (Community Learning and Information Network) *National Initiative Proposal*

CUE (Computer Using Educators, Inc) *Newsletter* September/October 1994

CUE (Computer Using Educators, Inc) *Educational Technology Legislative Update* 15.9.94

A Collection of Papers on Self-Study and Institutional Improvement, North Central Association of Colleges and Schools 1993

Congress of the United States Office of Technology Assessment *Publications Catalogue*

Cradler, J Comprehensive *Study of Educational Technology Programs in California Authorised from 1984–92* (Executive Summary), Far West Laboratory

Cradler, J *Planning for Technology Applications in Education*, Far West Laboratory

Cradler, J *Summary of Current Research and Evaluation Findings on Technology in Education*, Far West Laboratory

Cradler, J *Technology Planning to Support Educational Reform*, Far West Laboratory

Cradler, J and Bridgforth, E *California and the National Information Infrastructure*, Far West Laboratory

Cradler, J and Bridgforth, E *Comparison of Educational Technology and Telecommunications Plans*, Far West Laboratory

Cradler, J and Bridgforth, E *Goals 2000: Educate America Act Technology in Education Reform* (leaflet), Far West Laboratory

Cradler, J et al. *Technology Planning for the Goals 2000 State Improvement Plan*

Cradler, J et al. *Comprehensive Study of Educational Technology Programs Authorised from 1989–1992 , Vol. 1 School-Based Educational Technology Grants* 1991

The Curriculum Network (leaflet)

Cutler & Co Telecommunications *The Pacific Link*, report for the Pacific Forum 1994

Dempsey, A *Education, Urban America and ME/U: The Education Network*, Jones Education Networks 1994

Dulchinos, D P 'Bringing Fiber Optics to America: The Cable Television Experience', *Fiber and Integrated Optics*, Vol. 11, 1992

The Education Infrastructure Funding Forum Report, Pacific Bell 1994

Education Summit Summary and Conclusions, California State Assembly 1994

Ehrmann, S E *Looking Backward: A Funder Looks at US Efforts to Use Technology to Transform Undergraduate Education*, The Annenberg/CPB Projects 1993

Ehrmann, S E *US Higher Education in 1998: Using Technologies to Meet the Triple Challenge*, The Annenberg/CPB Projects 1993

'The End of School', *Popular Science*, January 1994

Feenberg, A *The Future of Teaching in the Planetary Classroom*, from the Proceedings of the 10th Annual Conference of the Pacific Region Association for Higher Education 1989

Gilbert, J A & Associates *Telecommunications in Support of Learning*, The Commonwealth of Learning 1993

Government of Canada Policy Initiative for the Information Superhighway (various documents)

Government Relations Handbook, National Council of Teachers of Mathematics 1994

Greene, S G 'Technology: Are Charities Missing the Revolution?' *The Chronicle of Philanthropy,* 19 October 1993

Harasim, L M 'Online Education: An Environment for Collaboration and Intellectual Amplification' in Harasim, L M (ed.) *Online Education,* Praeger Publishers, New York, 1990

Harasim, L M *Teaching and Learning Online: Issues in Computer-Mediated Graduate Courses,* CJEC Spring 1987

Hawaii Wide Area Integrated Information Network System Services (diagram)

Hawaii Research and Education Network Preliminary Proposal, Hawaii State Department of Education, University of Hawaii, East-West Center, Hawaii Information Network Consortium

Hedegaard, T 'Learning Online and on Campus: A Comparison of Adult Students' Professional Attitudes and Values', *ED Journal,* Vol. 8, No. 8

Henry, T 'Mind Extension University Brings College to Adults', *USA Today,* 14 March 1994

Home Study Marketing Survey, National Home Study Council (now Distance Education and Training Council) 1993

Improving Student Performance through Learning Technologies, Council of Chief State School Officers Policy Statement 1991

InfoActive, The Center for Media Education June, July 1994

The Information Superhighway and the Reinvention of Television, Center for Media Education

Information Superhighway Could Bypass Low Income and Minority Communities, Center for Media Education News Release 23 May 1994

Johnstone, S M *Evaluation of the Annenberg/CPB Projects' New Pathways to a Degree* (Executive Summary), Western Cooperative for Educational Telecommunications 1994

Jussawalla, Meheroo, list of publications

Kernan, J T *Summary of Testimony before the Subcommittee on Telecommunications and Finance* 1994

Lewis, C T and Hedegaard, T 'Online Education: Issues and Some Answers', *The Journal*, April 1993

Lohr, S 'Data Highway Ignoring Poor, Study Charges', *The New York Times*, 24 May 1994

Markoff, J 'New Coalition to Seek A Public Data Highway', *The New York Times*, 26 October 1993

Medium Costs to Establish a Telecommunications Infrastructure for a 27-Classroom School, California Department of Education Research, Evaluation and Technology Division 1994

Murray, C *The Canadian Network on Trade, Innovation, Competitiveness and Sustainability* (executive summary), Simon Fraser University

The National Information Infrastructure: Agenda for Action (executive summary)

National Information Infrastructure Public Policy White Paper, United States Telephone Association 1994

The National Information Infrastructure: Requirements for Education and Training, National Coordinating Committee on Technology in Education and Training 1994

National Telecommunications and Information Administration Telecommunications and Information Infrastructure Assistance Program Availability of Funds, United States Department of Commerce

An Overview of Telecommunications and Technology Activities, The Commonwealth of Learning 1993

Pacific Transit Cable Initiative (leaflet), Pacific Telecommunications Council 1993

Pan-Pacific Education and Communication Experiments by Satellite, PEACESAT leaflet

PEACESAT Services Improvement Plan

Piller, C *Dreamnet: Shattering Consumers' Illusions of the Information Superhighway*, Macworld Special Report October 1994

Power On, Congress of the United States Office of Technology Assessment 1988

Public Interest Groups Establish Consumer 'Highway Patrol' for the Information Superhighway, Center for Media Education/Consumer Federation of America 8 March 1994

Putting the Information Infrastructure to Work, National Institute of Standards and Technology United States Department of Commerce

Ramirez, R and Bell, R *Byting Back: Policies to Support the Use of Technology in Education*, North Central Regional Educational Laboratory 1994

Riley, R W (Secretary of Education) *Testimony before the Committee on Commerce, Science, and Transportation*, United States Senate 1994

Rothstein R I *Connecting K-12 Schools to the NII: A Preliminary Assessment of Technology Models and their Associated Costs*, US Department of Education Working Paper 1994

Rural America at the Crossroads: Networking for the Future, Congress of the United States Office of Technology Assessment 1991

Simpson, R J *Telecommunications and Distance Education: A Model for Small States*, paper given at International Institute of Communications Annual Conference 1993

Simpson, R J *Telecommunications Development and Education: Networks as Social Infrastructure*, The Commonwealth of Learning

Simpson, R J *Mixed Media – Open Networks – New Paradigms for Distance Learning*, The Commonwealth of Learning 1993

Simpson, R J *The Evolution of Markets for Multi-Media in Canada*, The Commonwealth of Learning

Technology 2000, State of Utah Initiative 1994

Trinational Institute on Innovation, Competitiveness and Sustainability (commissioned papers), Simon Fraser University

Universal Service and the Information Superhighway, The Benton Foundation

United States Advisory Council on the National Information Infrastructure (list of members)

What People Think About New Communications Technologies, The Benton Foundation

The Author

Keith Yeomans is an independent specialist in the development of electronic communications for education, training and public service. He has carried out strategic research, evaluative and feasibility studies for, among others, the BBC, British Telecom, the Commonwealth Secretariat, Dentsu Inc and several UK Government departments on the development of cross-sectoral electronic learning strategies, local public service communications environments, programming, finance and training in the media industry.

He has also worked extensively with the UK voluntary sector, preparing and evaluating communication strategies using social action broadcasting and the new media.

His international experience includes a study tour of development communications and media training in Australia, India, New Zealand, Singapore and Sri Lanka, facilitated by a Commonwealth Relations Trust bursary; a US Government-sponsored study tour of NGOs and the media in the United States; contributions to international conferences in Africa and Europe and to a Unesco training programme at the Asian Institute for Broadcasting Development in Malaysia; recent visits to Japan and Singapore to make a documentary for BBC World Service Radio on intelligent cities.

Keith Yeomans worked for 10 years in BBC radio and television production, where he developed several innovative partnership projects in community education. He also trained broadcasters with the British Council before leaving in 1980 to help set up the National Broadcasting School.

He lectures, writes and broadcasts on communications topics, is a member of the International Institute of Communications and a Fellow of the Royal Society for the Encouragement of Arts, Manufactures and Commerce.

He has a long-standing commitment to developing ways of using electronic communications to widen access to learning, especially for disadvantaged groups, both in the UK and in poorer countries.